Accountable Discipleship

Living in God's Household

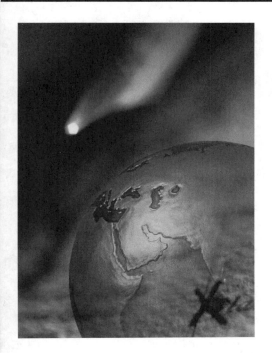

Steven W. Manskar

DISCIPLESHIP RESOURCES

P.O. BOX 340003 • NASHVILLE, TN 37203-0003
www.discipleshipresources.org

For Gina and Noah

We know love by this, that he laid down his life for us—and we ought to lay down our lives for one another. How does God's love abide in anyone who has the world's goods and sees a brother or sister in need and yet refuses help? Little children, let us love, not in word or speech, but in truth and action.
(1 John 3:16-18)

Cover and book design by Joey McNair
Edited by Debra D. Smith and Heidi L. Hewitt

Reprint 2006

ISBN 0-88177-339-5

Library of Congress Catalog Card No. 00-104478

DR339

Contents

Foreword

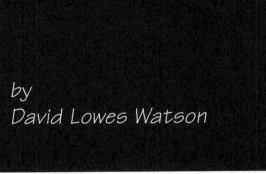

by
David Lowes Watson

One of the most significant and heartening developments for
Methodism in recent decades has been the renewed interest in the
life and ministry of John Wesley. In this very revival of Wesleyan studies, however, there is a pitfall. When given the attention they deserve,
the writings of Wesley—and the hymns of his brother Charles—emerge
as such a forceful course correction to the theology of the Reformation
that studying the writings easily can become a distraction from the
evangelical mission to which both brothers gave so much of their lives.
To avoid this pitfall, the academic pursuit of Wesleyan theology and history must be matched, if not exceeded, by studies that apply the
Wesleyan corpus to the practice of Christian discipleship in the world.

This is what makes Steven W. Manskar's contribution so critical and
so timely. His research into the Wesleys, John in particular, has been
grounded in a faithful application of the General Rules of 1743. To find
the General Rules today, one must look in the doctrinal paragraphs of *The
Book of Discipline of The United Methodist Church,* where they are pre-
ceded by accounts of our doctrinal heritage, history, and standards, and
are followed by our theological task. When first published, the General
Rules were intended as a practical guide to Christian living, a small penny
pamphlet to be carried around in the pocket, making the commandments

of Jesus altogether unavoidable. But today, sandwiched between doctrine and theology in a weighty *Book of Discipline*, they all too often can conveniently be consigned to the occasional reference.

With volumes such as Manskar's *Accountable Discipleship* in circulation, this is much less likely to happen. The subtitle of the book tells us where we are headed: *Living in God's Household.* The imagery is powerful and the narrative impelling as Chapter 1 confronts us with a question that frequently is avoided in our present North-American climate of personalized faith and privatized discipleship: What happens when we have accepted Christ's invitation to come home? Is there to be a continuous, unending welcome party, or must we wake up the next morning and find that living in God's household means accepting God's house rules?

Manskar tells us, in his down-to-earth, matter-of-fact Prologue, that he has faced this question directly for quite some time; that he has practiced mutual accountability in a Covenant Discipleship Group since his seminary days; that this has given him an insight into Wesley's theology that fuses faith and works into nonnegotiable habits and disciplines; and that pristine Methodism, whatever the origins of the nickname, continues to affirm and merit this derisive characterization precisely because of the way our spiritual forebears followed the commandments of Christ.

Manskar also assures us that the question remains discomforting for him. It certainly discomforts us as we are led through a series of biblical explorations that serve as an admirable introductory course in discipleship. Drawing on the best of contemporary scholarship, Manskar reminds us of the reality of the covenant with God into which Christ invites and empowers us. This is the God who brought the Hebrews out of slavery, who thundered the Law from Sinai, whose prophets made kings tremble, and who was fully revealed in Jesus of Nazareth, the Christ. Our response to this covenant-making God must therefore be as particular as the commandments of the young Jewish rabbi who was born in Bethlehem, grew up in Galilee, taught, healed, and embodied God's love to the point of rejection and execution by a sinful world. His commandments are authoritative because God raised him from the dead, "highly exalted him and gave him the name that is above every name" (Philippians 2:9).

In providing us with such clear scriptural referents, Manskar also shows us why Wesley's theology and polity are so compelling for the church today. If we are indeed members of the household of God and take seriously the mutual responsibility this enjoins on all household members, then we cannot regard God's house rules as merely the overflow of parental good nature, to be followed with minimum effort on our part and maximum divine condescension. Rather, these rules are the condition of living in God's household. If we have accepted God's invitation to come home, and if we have enjoyed the celebrations of the coming-home party, then we also must accept the obligations. If we wish to remain in God's household, then we are commanded to love God and to love one another. And that is that.

Perhaps the most insightful part of this book is its interpretive account of Wesley's theology of discipleship. Eschewing recent criticisms of the Wesleyan quadrilateral, Manskar demonstrates through the fourfold method of Scripture, tradition, reason, and experience that the key to Wesley's theology of discipleship is his doctrine of justification.

For those of us schooled in the significance of prevenient and sanctifying grace, to say nothing of Christian perfection, this is a refreshing spring that wondrously clears the muddied waters of faith and works.

In true Wesleyan tradition, Manskar explains in plain words for plain people how the Reformation doctrine of justification had become overloaded with a forensic formality it was never meant to carry. Justification merely begins our discipleship; sanctification shapes it. Justification is the ongoing dynamic of our life in God's household; sanctification is the development of our obedience to the house rules. Without this distinction, we tend inexorably toward one of the two extremes that ultimately enervate Christian discipleship: on the one hand, an undue emphasis on our relationship with Christ, which places us on the slippery slope of self-deception; on the other hand, an undue emphasis on working for Christ in the world, which undermines the relational grounding of discipleship implied in the word *obedience.*

Accountable Discipleship, then, provides us with the practical guidelines needed for walking with Christ in the world. We are given a taste of Methodist history sufficiently rich to whet the appetite for further exploration, and sufficiently contextual for us to realize that we cannot use our spiritual heritage as a way of avoiding the challenges of our own day. In coming home, we cannot just go back home. We cannot recover the methods of early Methodism without traditioning them—that is, appropriating the methods of our forebears, not merely copying them. In advocating the role of Covenant Discipleship Groups and class leaders in the church of today, Manskar does not fall into the trap of seeking the end without the means. Yes, there are significant lessons for us in our Wesleyan heritage, but we must follow the example of our forebears and play our part in applying the lessons. For if there is one thing that the early Methodists demonstrate, on both sides of the Atlantic, it is their driving concern to be obedient to Jesus Christ in the present. Memory can shape our discipleship, but it must not stifle the immediacy of our response.

Two further insights are afforded by Manskar's own discipleship. The first insight is a passion for Christ's imperative to know and serve the poor, and to let them know and serve us. There could be no better example of how to take the basics of Wesley's General Rules, and in turn the General Rule of Discipleship ("To witness to Jesus Christ in the world, and to follow his teachings through acts of compassion, justice, worship, and devotion, under the guidance of the Holy Spirit"), and apply them to particular acts of compassion, justice, worship, and devotion. If we have not fed the hungry, clothed the naked, visited the prisoners, and tended the sick, then we can expect rigorous evaluation in eternity. If Manskar comes across as harsh in this regard, he merely echoes Wesley, and Jesus himself, whose call to discipleship was blunt and often brutal (Luke 14:25-27).

The second insight is Manskar's concern for clarity of focus around the role of lay leadership in the church. Of all major Protestant denominations, United Methodism alone lacks a well-defined lay office, which is the equivalent of the Baptist deacon, the Presbyterian elder, the Disciples lay elder, to name but three. By contrast, we have job descriptions in The United Methodist Church. This may be one of the penalties of Wesley's Anglican heritage, even though he himself was constantly at pains to affirm the role of leaders and stewards in the Methodist societies. In *Accountable Discipleship* we have a glimpse of an office that might yet be recovered from our Methodist heritage.

It is fitting that this book should appear shortly after Manskar has assumed the portfolio for Accountable Discipleship at the General Board of Discipleship. It confirms not only that this ministry is timely and crucial for The United Methodist Church, and indeed for the church at large, but also that the right person has been called to lead it.

Dr. David Lowes Watson helped develop and organize the first Covenant Discipleship Groups in 1975. Since that time he has been a leader in the field of Accountable Discipleship, helping countless congregations begin Covenant Discipleship Groups.

Prologue

Accountable Discipleship: My Story

Accountable Discipleship has been an important part of my life since 1989, when I entered Wesley Theological Seminary as a student pastor. Every student at Wesley participates, as a requirement for graduation, in a Covenant Discipleship Group. The rationale is that leaders for the church need to be formed spiritually and equipped intellectually and technically for ministry. The concept of being accountable for my formation as a disciple and leader appealed to me. It was after arriving at Wesley that I learned that accountability in small groups was an important part of the United Methodist heritage and theology.

I was in a Covenant Discipleship Group three of my four years at Wesley. My experience in those groups convinced me of the importance of mutual accountability and support for the formation of leaders for the church. The groups helped me grow in my relationship with Christ. As I paid closer attention to my walk with Christ, I grew in my understanding of my own strengths and weaknesses with regard to my discipleship and call to ministry. Covenant Discipleship was one of the most important parts of my theological education.

Another thing Covenant Discipleship Groups do, in a seminary or in a congregation, is to help in the building of community. One of the purposes of Covenant Discipleship Groups is to help people grow closer to God. A consequence of weekly accountability and prayer support from group members is that each person is helped to nurture his or her relationship to God. As people grow closer to God, they also grow closer to one another. This probably is one of the reasons Jesus told us the greatest commandment: " 'You shall love the Lord your God with all your heart, and with all your soul, and with all your mind.'... And a second is like it: 'You shall love your neighbor as yourself' " (Matthew 22:37, 39). This also is reflected in 1 John 4:7-9: "Beloved, let us love one another, because love is from God; everyone who loves is born of God and knows God. Whoever does not love does not know God, for God is love. God's love was revealed among us in this way: God sent his only Son into the world so that we might live through him."

Covenant Discipleship simply helps people love God and love their neighbor. To love God is to love the neighbor, and to love the neighbor is to love God. As people grow in their love for God, for one another, and for their neighbor, Christian community is built, nurtured, and strengthened. This is the love of Jesus Christ that is alive and living in and through people as they strive to follow him. Because of this dynamic, Covenant Discipleship Groups are an essential part of community life at Wesley Theological Seminary.

My experience in seminary convinced me of the importance of Accountable Discipleship for the mission and ministry of the local church. I have started Covenant Discipleship Groups in every church I have served as pastor. I had three reasons for establishing the groups:
1. Covenant Discipleship Groups form and shape disciples.
2. Covenant Discipleship Groups form and support leaders for the church.
3. Covenant Discipleship Groups help pastors grow in their own discipleship, which results in more-effective pastors.

My mission and primary responsibility as a pastor was to proclaim the good news of God in Jesus Christ and to teach those who responded how to live as his disciples in their daily lives. First, Covenant Discipleship Groups are the most effective means of forming the discipleship of those who are willing to be accountable and to give and receive the support of their peers. The groups I have experienced have changed individual lives through the intentionality of the covenant and the accountability of the group. Group members become more-active participants and leaders in worship. They find ways to serve within the church and the community. Their lives, which are centered on Christ, touch the lives of many others who experience Christ in new ways through a comforting word or gesture, an act of compassion at a time of need, or a challenging word spoken in the name of justice and for the common good. Covenant Discipleship provides the structure that helps people know what it means to follow Jesus, and it empowers them to act accordingly.

Second, Covenant Discipleship Groups often reveal gifts for leadership that live within many disciples. It models a healthy, Christ-centered leadership that is focused on serving people's needs, mutual accountability, and prayer. The accountability and prayer support given and received in groups equip leaders for ministry. The groups help keep the leaders' focus on Christ, subduing the temptation toward serving themselves and keeping them focused on serving Christ in the world.

Third, Covenant Discipleship Groups help pastors grow in their personal discipleship, which makes them better, more-effective pastors. The group process with laypeople from the local church helps keep the pastor's attention and ministry focused on making the good news of Jesus Christ good news indeed for everyone by helping to keep the pastor's life centered in Christ.

Covenant Discipleship Groups have been an essential part of my life. I could not have been a faithful, effective pastor without the accountability and support I have received from brothers and sisters in Christ at West Liberty United Methodist Church in White Hall, Maryland; Preston and Lanesboro United Methodist Churches in southeastern Minnesota; and Chester Park United Methodist Church in Duluth, Minnesota. The people in those churches helped form me as a disciple of Jesus Christ and as a pastor. The love and support I received from Christ through them gave me direction and purpose in my ministry among them, helped me serve them more faithfully, and made me a better pastor.

This book flows from my experience with Accountable Discipleship in the seminary and in the local church. Writing this book has been a daunting task. I am indebted to the members of the Council for Accountable Discipleship for the love and support I have received. I give thanks to James C. Logan for introducing me to John and Charles Wesley, M. Douglas Meeks for opening my eyes to seeing God as the one who makes home for and with us, Bruce Birch for helping me understand more fully the connection between Scripture and daily living, and Douglas Strong for his insight into the history of our spiritual ancestors and mentors in discipleship and faith. David Lowes Watson has been, and continues to be, a mentor and friend to me. His work has helped form me as a disciple and as a pastor. I can never thank him adequately for the love and support he gave me during the writing of this book. Finally, to my wife and son, Gina and Noah, I give thanks for their love and most of all for their enduring patience, without which I could never have completed this project. They are a blessing to me for which I give thanks every day.

I pray that this book will illuminate and increase your understanding of Accountable Discipleship. May God bless your life and ministry.

Chapter 1

Accountable Discipleship: Living in God's Household

The parable of the prodigal son (Luke 15:11-32) is a story of grace. In it Jesus teaches us about God's unconditional, unmerited love for God's own children. The parable resonates with people because it is a story about a family and their struggles to live together in love. The story includes betrayal, unconditional love, and forgiveness, along with bitterness and resentment. In this parable we find a picture of God and God's way of love for God's children. We see God as the head of a household, who loves and forgives and holds the family together. As we read the parable, we experience that love and are inspired to live our lives accordingly. This is the beginning of Accountable Discipleship.

The following is a retelling of the parable of the prodigal son:

Jesus begins, "There was a man who had two sons." The younger son went to dear old dad and demanded his share of the inheritance. To everyone's surprise, the old man gave into the son's demands and handed over the money. The young man immediately left home and headed for a distant land, where he spent all the money on wine, women, and song. When the cash was gone, so were his friends. Broke, homeless, humiliated, and with no prospects for the future, the younger son took a job feeding the pigs of a local farmer. One day he found himself so hungry that he could have eaten the slop he was giving the pigs. His hunger and humiliation helped him to wake up to what he had done and how far he had fallen. With a belly growling for food, the kid started thinking about home and how his father's servants were treated well and always had plenty to eat. He thought, *Maybe I could go home and be one of my dad's farm hands.* So he got up and started toward home. Along the way he practiced a speech he was going to give to his dad: "Father, I have sinned against heaven and before you. I am no longer worthy to be called your son; treat me like one of your hired hands."

Jesus goes on to tell us about the welcome the younger son received when he finally arrived at the family homestead: As the younger son walked up the driveway, the old man amazed him by running out to greet him, with his arms outstretched. It was a warm and moving moment for the two men. Both shed tears of joy. As the son was trying to give his speech of remorse, the old man began shouting orders to the servants to bring a new robe and the family ring and to make preparations for a big welcome-home party. Before he knew what had hit him, the son was dressed in his father's finest robe, the family ring was on his finger, and he was the guest of honor at a sumptuous feast of fine food and wine.

The party stretched well into the night, and a good time was had by all. The father made clear to his younger son that he was overjoyed that he had returned to take his rightful place in the family. His son, whom he had given up for dead, now was alive. The one he thought was lost had been found. The only appropriate response to such a joy was a great feast of celebration.

But not everyone agreed. Enter the older son. He was the dependable one, the guy who always was there pulling his weight, the responsible one. When his kid brother took off, he did his own work and found a way to get his brother's work done as well. Now his brother was back, and the old man was throwing a party for him! The older brother refused to join in the celebration. His father went out to talk to him and got an earful.

"Listen! For all these years I have been working like a slave for you, and I never have disobeyed your command. Yet you never have given me even a young goat so that I might celebrate with my friends. But you killed the fatted calf when this son of yours, who has devoured your property with prostitutes, came back!"

The father absorbed his son's tirade. He looked into his eyes and said, "Son, you are always with me, and all that is mine is yours. But we had to celebrate and rejoice, because this brother of yours was dead and has come to life; he was lost and has been found."

That's where Jesus ends his story. The point is that God's love is like the love of the father: God welcomes us back with open arms. God's love is unconditional. When a sinner returns to God's household, God's impulse is to throw a big, blowout party. God and God's household celebrate each life that is restored to its rightful place at God's table. (See Luke 15:1-10.)

There is more to the story. What if Jesus were to add another chapter, called "The Morning After"? The chapter would begin the morning after the celebration of the younger brother's return to his father's home, the home he had turned his back on and dishonored.

It was five in the morning and was still dark outside. The younger brother was sound asleep in his bed after a long night of eating and drinking. There was a loud knock on his bedroom door. No answer. A louder knock. This time he stumbled out of bed and opened the door. He was greeted by his older brother, the guy who was so angry with him that he would not join in the previous evening's festivities. This time the older brother had a grin on his face as he told his brother, "It's after five in the morning! It's time to get to work. Dad and I have been carrying your load around here while you were off having a good time. Now it's time you started carrying your own weight. There's plenty of work to be done. Let's get at it! Oh, and by the way, welcome home, brother!"

The younger brother, while he was happy to be back home, had forgotten about the responsibilities that go along with life in his father's household. There was work to be done every day, and everyone had a job to do. It was time for him to get to work, to pick up where he had left off when he had departed so suddenly. His brother was happy to remind him that living in their father's house meant living by the household rules.

Accountable Discipleship

Accountable Discipleship is a distinctively Methodist way of Christian formation. Its origins are found in the movement led by John and Charles Wesley, priests in the Church of England whose lives spanned most of the eighteenth century. It was a time of great social and economic change and turmoil, as the Industrial Revolution was beginning. Many poor people migrated from the country to the towns and cities, where they hoped to find jobs in the mills, factories, and mines. The Wesleys and others (such as George Whitefield) saw that the Church of England was not reaching the working poor. The lives of thousands of men, women, and children were virtually untouched by the good news of Jesus Christ. John Wesley was motivated by his study of the Bible to imitate his Savior and do what he could to bring good news to the poor, feed the hungry, give water to the thirsty, clothe the naked, visit the sick and imprisoned, and welcome the stranger. Wesley devoted himself to bringing the gospel of Christ to the people who were most open to receiving it, the same people the established church had neglected. He helped those who responded to his preaching and teaching by using what is known today as Accountable Discipleship.

For many years John Wesley traveled the English countryside on horseback. He preached in cities, towns, and hamlets throughout the land. He organized societies everywhere people responded to his message of God's good news for the world in Jesus Christ. A Methodist society was comparable to a local church of today. It was a group of people who had been moved by the Holy Spirit to respond to the invitation to give their lives to Jesus Christ. The societies were divided into smaller groups, called classes, that had up to twelve people. Women and men with experience in the Christian life were instructed by Wesley and given the responsibility to lead a class. They were known as class leaders. The classes met weekly to pray, sing, and read the Bible together. Everyone was given the opportunity by the leader to tell how he or she had walked with Christ since the last meeting. The purpose of the class meeting was to "watch over one another in love." Those small groups were the organizational force that powered the Methodist portion of the Evangelical revival that swept England and America in the eighteenth century.

Covenant Discipleship, today's entry point for Accountable Discipleship, is an adaptation of the early Methodist class meetings. It is not an attempt to re-create an eighteenth-century model and apply it to the twenty-first century. In Covenant Discipleship we have lifted out the pieces of the class meeting that are most needed for Christians of today: mutual accountability and support. While elements of the class meeting, such as prayer and Bible reading, are recommended components, they are not the main thing. The purpose of Covenant Discipleship is accountability, which is where people come to give an account of their daily walk with Christ. It is where people listen, ask questions, and support and help one another as they are formed as disciples of Jesus Christ. Accountability is distinctive to Covenant Discipleship because disciples need the encouragement and support it affords.

It is important to understand that when we say accountability, we are not implying or encouraging a form of judgment or works righteousness. The accountability of Covenant Discipleship is simply giving an account of how one has lived his or her life in light of a covenant created by his or her Covenant Discipleship Group. Telling others how your week has gone, what you have done, and what you have not done helps one check in with the group, with themselves, and with the one who counts most, Jesus Christ. Giving an account of the week helps clarify the areas of strength and of weakness. The strengths can be affirmed and perhaps can provide inspiration to others in the group. The areas of weakness reveal places where prayer, support, and encouragement may be given. They also indicate where growth is most likely to take place. In the process, each member is formed as a disciple of Jesus Christ. Accountability helps keep those willing to engage in it moving forward with Christ.

Discipleship

Discipleship is the way of living that follows the life and teachings of Jesus Christ. A disciple is one who follows and learns from a teacher. Disciples of Jesus Christ are people who respond to his call on their lives to come follow him (Matthew 4:18-22). He is the one who has chosen and called us in baptism. Disciples follow Jesus, learn from him, and do their best to obey his commandments: "Love your enemies and pray for those who persecute you" (Matthew 5:44); "You shall love the Lord your God with all your heart, and with all your soul, and with all your mind.... You shall love your neighbor as yourself" (Matthew 22:37, 39); "Love one another. Just as I have loved you, you also should love one another" (John 13:34).

A disciple learns by spending time with the teacher; therefore, the disciple needs to go where the teacher goes. Because Jesus is our teacher, we need to go to the places he is most likely to be living today. Where is Jesus alive today?

To answer this question, let us look at the Bible. On several occasions the religious leaders of Jesus' day complained because Jesus "welcomes sinners and eats with them" (Luke 15:2). "The Pharisees and their scribes were complaining to his disciples, saying, 'Why do you eat and drink with tax collectors and sinners?' Jesus answered, 'Those who are well have no need of a physician, but those who are sick; I have come to call not the righteous but sinners to repentance'" (Luke 5:30-32). Where in your community will you find those the Gospel writers called tax collectors and sinners? They were the outcasts, the marginalized, the despised, the disposable people of the community. And they were the ones with whom Jesus identified himself: "Truly I tell you, just as you did it to one of the least of these who are members of my family, you did it to me" (Matthew 25:40). Today, disciples will find the people with whom Jesus identified himself in places such as soup kitchens, unemployment offices, jails, prisons, hospitals, nursing homes, homeless shelters, drop-in centers, plasma centers, bus stations, doorways, and any place the poor, despised, vulnerable, voiceless, and marginalized people of today are found—even churches. Disciples learn by following their teacher and serving in the places where he lives and works.

The goal of discipleship is to form people into the image of Christ, to "let the same mind be in you that was in Christ Jesus" (Philippians 2:5). Discipleship is the life we live with Christ and with our fellow disciples as members of Christ's body in the world, the church. It is important for us to understand that discipleship is not an individual, Jesus-and-me relationship. Being a disciple means, by its very nature, living as a member of a community of other disciples. It means participating in the life of Christ as a member of his body (1 Corinthians 12:12-14). Disciples need to be part of the church because that is where they learn about their teacher through the lives of other disciples, through hearing his word proclaimed in worship and in Bible study. The church is where disciples participate in and receive the grace conveyed by the sacraments of baptism and the Lord's Supper. Finally, disciples need to live in community with other disciples because they need to be accountable to someone other than themselves for their discipleship.

Discipleship is how the church fulfills its mission in the world. If the church is to live out its mission faithfully, the disciples who are the bearers of that mission need to be accountable to one another. One of the great temptations of faithful discipleship is self-deception. Disciples of Jesus Christ are also human beings who are sinners. They are vulnerable to the temptations of self-righteousness and self-centeredness. Regular mutual accountability is a means of preventing self-deception and keeping our discipleship aligned with Christ. Faithful discipleship builds up the church by building up disciples.

Finally, discipleship is the way of life in God's household. We will explore the nature of God's household in more detail in Chapter 3. The call to follow Jesus is an invitation to life in the household of God. Accepting the call to discipleship is acceptance of adoption into God's family (Romans 8:14-17; Galatians 4:4-7; Ephesians 1:3-14; 2:19-22). As members of God's household, disciples are sisters and brothers to one another. Jesus is their mentor and brother. As God's adopted children, disciples are Christ's representatives in the world (2 Corinthians 5:20). As God's adopted children and Christ's representatives, disciples have a responsibility to live lives that are a reflection of their parent and their brother. Discipleship is the way of God's household. It is God's way of compassion, justice, righteousness, and steadfast love. It is following Jesus in such a way that others are invited into the household, and acting in ways that honor the parent and the parent's desire for the welfare of the whole of creation. The word that best describes the nature of this discipleship is *covenant.*

Covenant

A covenant is a relationship initiated by God, signed and sealed by God with the blood of God's Son, to deliver humankind from the powers of sin and death. Discipleship is the human response to this covenant of love, the unconditional love of God, incarnate in Jesus Christ, for humankind; and the love of human beings for God and one another. It is a covenant in which God has given God's self in the life, death, and resurrection of Jesus Christ in order to restore *shalom* to human lives and community. *Shalom*, a Hebrew word that encompasses God's intended will for all of creation, means "wholeness, harmony, completeness, and peace." Jesus Christ is the incarnation of this covenant, this shalom. The human response to his gracious initiative is to turn our lives Godward. Discipleship is living out the Godward life. It is living in the covenant, the divine-human relationship of forgiveness, reconciliation, healing, wholeness—in other words, grace.

Covenant is God's way of being and acting in relation to humankind. It is a relationship initiated by God for and with human beings and human communities. An important element of covenant is the making and keeping of promises. For example, in the covenant with Abraham and Sarah (Genesis 15), God promised land (a place to call home), heirs (home with a future), and new identity (blessed to be a blessing). Abraham's part of the covenant was to trust and follow God. If you have read Abraham's story (Genesis 12:1–25:18), you know that God kept all of God's promises in the covenant made with Abraham. God led him and his family to the Promised Land; Sarah gave birth, in her old age, to a son, Isaac; and both Abraham and Sarah were given new names. Abraham and Sarah's part in the covenant was to trust God and to go, to follow. Anyone who has read their story knows that Abraham and Sarah were not perfectly obedient participants of the covenant. They made mistakes and missteps along the way; but, because of the covenant, God forgave them and did not give up on them. And, because God never gave up on them, they did not give up on themselves. Because God was faithful, they could become faithful. By their obedience to God and the covenant, Abraham and Sarah became the father and mother of many nations.

Another important covenant that helps us understand discipleship is the covenant made at Sinai with Moses and the Hebrew people (Exodus 3:4–4:17). After delivering the people from slavery in Egypt, leading them to freedom across the sea into the wilderness, God gave Moses the Ten Commandments (Exodus 20:1-17). The commandments are the covenant through which a band of refugee slaves became a nation. They are the foundation of a community established by God to be a light to the nations, a light of righteousness and justice that would reveal the power and nature of God to all the nations of the world. The commandments established the rules for life in God's household. Their purpose was to assure that all members of the household got what they needed to live.

The covenant at Sinai contains a promise of loyalty and a commitment to preserving human life and community. The promise of loyalty is mutual. God, in the giving of the covenant, promises God's eternal faithfulness to God's people. God will be their God, and they will be God's people. It is clear that God never breaks a promise; God always keeps God's word. There is nothing a people can do that will prevent God from fulfilling God's promises to them. The covenant at Sinai begins with God's first words to Moses: "I am the God of your father, the God of Abraham, the God of Isaac, and the God of Jacob."

It continues in Exodus 3:7-8:

> I have observed the misery of my people who are in Egypt; I have heard their cry on account of their taskmasters. Indeed, I know their sufferings, and I have come down to deliver them from the Egyptians, and to bring them up out of that land to a good and broad land, a land flowing with milk and honey.

This is the God who identifies with the oppressed, sees their misery, and hears their cries. This is the God who knows. In Hebrew, *to know* is relational more than it is cognitive and encompasses all the ways one knows and relates to another. It is entering into intimate relationship, sharing fully the life of the one who is known, and experiencing one with another. Knowing makes God vulnerable, open to being wounded. This God opens God's self to suffering, becoming vulnerable to the point of sharing in human suffering: "He was wounded for our transgressions,…and by his wounds we are healed" (Isaiah 53:5). God's eternal loyalty to God's people is expressed in God's knowing. For as God knows us, God will never forget or forsake us. God always will be God.

God gave the Ten Commandments in order to give the people a means for living out their part of the covenant. The first four commandments help God's people know how to live out their loyalty to their creator and deliverer. The commandments begin with the reminder of who God is and what God has done: "I am the LORD your God, who brought you out of the land of Egypt, out of the house of slavery; you shall have no other gods before me" (Exodus 20:2-3). There can be no mistake as to which God the people are called to give their loyalty. The second, third, and fourth commandments (not worshiping idols, not wrongfully using God's name, and remembering and keeping the sabbath) help the people know how to live with this God who has delivered them from slavery. The remaining six commandments (honoring parents, not murdering, not committing adultery, not stealing, not lying, and not coveting) set the foundation for basic human rights. They establish the framework in which the people may live in freedom as God's children, members of God's household. These household members are free to honor their parents, to live without fear, to have fidelity in marriage, to be secure in their property, to tell the truth, and to live without covetousness. God's commandments are a declaration of freedom on which life in God's household is established. Those who accept God's call and enter the household know the household rules.

Jesus summarized the commandments when he was asked by the scribes which of the commandments was the greatest:

> Jesus answered, "The first is, 'Hear, O Israel: the Lord our God, the Lord is one; you shall love the Lord your God with all your heart, and with all your soul, and with all your mind, and with all your strength.' The second is this, 'You shall love your neighbor as yourself.' There is no other commandment greater than these." (Mark 12:29-31)

Jesus recapitulates the covenant in terms of love. Jesus is the covenant come to life in flesh and blood. His life is the covenant acted out for all to see. In Jesus Christ God gives God's very self in order to draw the world to God. Jesus is the incarnation of the God who knows human suffering and oppression created by sin. The covenant offered to all the world in Jesus, sealed with his blood on the cross and ratified in his resurrection, calls those who accept the call to come and follow. He calls people to turn away from the false promises of the world that lead to death and to turn toward the promises of God and life in God's kingdom.

In Jesus the God who knows calls his disciples to be people who remember:

> The Lord Jesus on the night when he was betrayed took a loaf of bread, and when he had given thanks, he broke it and said, "This is my body that is for you. Do this in remembrance of me." In the same way he took the cup also, after supper, saying, "This cup is the new covenant in my blood. Do this, as often as you drink it, in remembrance of me." (1 Corinthians 11:23-25)

This remembering means more than cognitive remembering of events. When Jesus tells his disciples to "do this in remembrance of me," he is telling them to live their lives as though he is with them. As they remember Jesus, the disciples are to order their lives in a way that assumes he is present and active in their world. Jesus is more than a pleasant memory; he is a present reality. Disciples remember Jesus in order to re-present him to the world in their own actions and words. As they remember Jesus in this way, disciples live out their covenant with him.

Baptism

Through the Sacrament of Baptism
  we are initiated into Christ's holy church.
We are incorporated into God's mighty acts of salvation
  and given new birth through water and the Spirit.
All this is God's gift, offered to us without price.
(From "Baptismal Covenant I," in *The United Methodist Hymnal,* page 33. © 1976, 1980, 1985, 1989 The United Methodist Publishing House. Used by permission.)

The introduction to the Baptismal Covenant in *The United Methodist Hymnal* describes the promises God gives to those who have received the waters of baptism. The Baptismal Covenant is the relationship that makes discipleship possible, for it binds us to God in Jesus Christ and to one another. Baptism is the covenant that marks the beginning of Christian discipleship. In baptism God claims us as God's own, grafts us into the body of Christ (the church), and promises always to love and forgive us.

Baptism is God's initiative. In the Baptismal Covenant, disciples receive the power of the Holy Spirit and the support and nurture of the community to live as children of God. Discipleship is the way God gives us to live out this covenant established at our baptism. It is the proper response to an amazing grace given at a high cost: the suffering, death, and resurrection of God's Son. The beginning of this covenant relationship is the cross. In it God, in Jesus Christ, suffered and died and on the third day rose again to destroy the powers of sin and death so that all the world might have eternal life: life with God in God's household.

Discipleship is the life worthy of such an awesome and life-giving grace. Because Christ has given himself to and for the world, we can give ourselves to him. In his life, death, and resurrection, we are forgiven, reconciled, loved unconditionally, and set free to love.

Covenant Discipleship

When we put covenant and discipleship together, we have a discipleship that is Christ-centered. It begins with Jesus who, by grace, calls disciples to come follow him. Grace awakens them to their own sinfulness, brokenness, and emptiness within their soul that they have not been able to fill. Grace helps them see that Christ is the only one who can fill that void in their lives. He is the source of forgiveness for their sins and healing for their brokenness. Christ draws them to himself and into community with others whom he has called. Covenant Discipleship is the way disciples live their lives in the world with Christ, for Christ, and for Christ's church.

Disciples learn about who Jesus is through Covenant Discipleship and by doing the things he told his disciples to do. His command to them can be summarized as love God and love your neighbor as you love yourself. Loving (self-giving, unconditional loving) is the essence of Christ and the life he calls each person to live. This loving is the living out of an amazing grace that transforms the disciple and changes the world in which he or she lives. Covenant Discipleship is the living out of the relationship with Christ through faithful obedience to God and God's commandments. It is life lived in and by grace.

Sin is a very real power in the world. Although disciples live in the grace of Christ, they remain vulnerable sinners. Becoming a disciple of Jesus Christ does not render you invulnerable to the power and temptations of sin. In fact, once a person says yes to Christ, the powers of sin and evil rally their forces to turn that yes into a no. That is why the apostle Paul instructed disciples to do the following:

> Be strong in the Lord and in the strength of his power. Put on the whole armor of God... For our struggle is not against enemies of blood and flesh, but against the rulers, against the authorities, against the cosmic powers of this present darkness, against the spiritual forces of evil.
> (Ephesians 6:10-12)

Disciples are vulnerable to self-deception, temptation, and distraction. The powers of the world constantly strive to deceive and tempt with the lure of materialism, narcissism, and greed in all their vulgar and subtle ways. God has given the church Covenant Discipleship as a means for helping them form disciples and resist the temptations of self-deception and self-centeredness.

Accountability

Accountability is how we make sure our discipleship happens. The primary task of Covenant Discipleship is to give disciples the means to prevent and resist the temptation to self-deception. Watching over one another in love helps disciples stand against the trap of believing and living as though they were self-sufficient (having all that is needed, in and of themselves, to be faithful to Christ's call). Mutual accountability prevents us from believing there is no need to "work out [our] own salvation" (Philippians 2:12). Covenant Discipleship also helps people resist the temptation to think they can be disciples when they feel like it, when it is convenient, when it feels good.

Finally, Covenant Discipleship works to prevent the inclination of humans to gravitate toward those things that they like to do and that are most attractive to them. It gives a model for a balanced, holistic discipleship. Because it is centered on Christ and his teachings, Covenant Discipleship addresses the needs of the whole person, not just the parts that are the most interesting or attractive. Covenant Discipleship is discipleship that is accountable to other disciples and to Christ. Its distinguishing characteristic is giving disciples the opportunity each week to give an account of their life with Christ in the world. Accountability, giving an account, is the key to preventing self-deception and the development of a lopsided discipleship.

The General Rule of Discipleship

Nothing can be more simple, nothing more rational, than the Methodist discipline: it is entirely founded on common sense, particularly applying the general rules of Scripture. Any person determined to save his soul may be united (this is the only condition required) with them. But this desire must be evidenced by three marks: avoiding all known sin, doing good after his power, and attending all the ordinances of God. He is then placed in such a class as is convenient for him, where he spends about an hour in a week. And the next quarter, if nothing is objected to him, he is admitted into the Society. And therein he may continue as long as he continues to meet his brethren and walks according to his profession.

(From "On God's Vineyard," in *The Works of John Wesley,* Volume 3, edited by Albert C. Outler, pages 511–12. © 1986 Abingdon Press. Used by permission.)

Near the end of his life, after visiting the Methodist societies of England and Wales, John Wesley wrote the sermon titled "On God's Vineyard," in which he recounted the origins, history, and practice of the Methodist movement. In the portion quoted above, he describes the simplicity and genius of the Methodist way of forming disciples. At the center of life among the societies and classes were the General Rules. The purpose of the General Rules was to provide guidance for the formation of Christian character among the members. The rules, which were based on the life and teachings of Jesus Christ, gave those who sought membership in the Methodist society a picture of what Christian discipleship looks like. The rules were like a compass heading for living that pointed people toward their destination. For the Methodists, the destination was holiness of heart and life.

The General Rules were simple:

First: By doing no harm, by avoiding evil of every kind, especially that which is most generally practiced...

Secondly: By doing good; by being in every kind merciful after their power; as they have opportunity, doing good of every possible sort, and, as far as is possible, to all men...

Thirdly: By attending upon all the ordinances of God; such are:
The public worship of God.
The ministry of the Word, either read or expounded.
The Supper of the Lord.
Family and private prayer.
Searching the Scriptures.
Fasting or abstinence.

(From *The Book of Discipline of The United Methodist Church—1996,* ¶ 62, pages 70–72. Copyright © 1996 by The United Methodist Publishing House. Used by permission.)

It must be said at the outset of the discussion of the General Rules that they are not intended to be a form of law. They are not a means for works righteousness (seeking to earn God's favor through good works). That has already been done for all the world by Christ, crucified and risen. These rules are intended to function as a rule for living, which is why they are called General Rules. They are meant to be broadly applied to meet the diverse needs of those who answer Christ's call to take up the cross and follow him (Luke 9:23). Wesley meant for them to be an encouragement for the Methodists, a goal set before them. Wesley believed they were a goal that could, by the grace of God, be attained.

The General Rules have within them the balanced, holistic approach that is necessary for the formation of faithful Christian character. In them is found a balance between what Wesley calls works of mercy and works of piety. The works of mercy are the avoiding of evil and the doing of good. The works of piety are "attending to the ordinances of God," or practicing the instituted means of grace. Works of mercy describe the things that are done in relation to the neighbor, while the works of piety describe the things that are done in personal relation to God. In other words, the General Rules point disciples in the direction they need to go if they are to live faithfully by the commandments of Christ: "You shall love the Lord your God with all your heart, and with all your soul, and with all your mind.... You shall love your neighbor as yourself" (Matthew 22:37, 39).

Thanks to the work of David Lowes Watson, we have a contemporary restatement of the General Rules. The General Rule of Discipleship maintains the Christ-centered, balanced, and varied approach to disciple formation given to the church by John Wesley: "To witness to Jesus Christ in the world, and to follow his teachings through acts of compassion, justice, worship, and devotion, under the guidance of the Holy Spirit."

The General Rule of Discipleship is open and broad. It is general in order to accommodate the varied experiences, interpretations, and perspectives disciples bring with them. The rule is not ideological and does not impose a narrow agenda or theological point of view. It is general precisely because Jesus' call to follow him is not limited or narrow. It is for all.

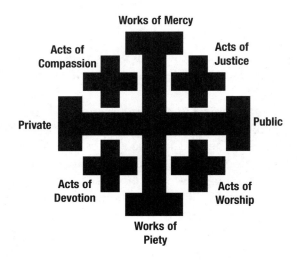

The General Rule of Discipleship begins with the idea that disciples are people who are witnesses to and for Jesus Christ in the world. A witness is someone who has an experience to share, a story to tell. Disciples share their experience of Jesus Christ by telling and participating in his story. "God so loved the world that he gave his only Son, so that everyone who believes in him may not perish but may have eternal life" (John 3:16). Disciples tell the good news of God's love for the world made flesh and blood in Jesus Christ by living as though Christ lived in them. They are living, by their words and actions, his continuing story of salvation, healing, wholeness, compassion, and justice (shalom) in their daily lives. They can live Christ's continuing story because they know his story given to the world in the Bible. Disciples are witnesses to Jesus Christ in the world. Their faith is integrated into their daily lives and is not limited to the confines of the church. They are the living, breathing body of Christ working in the world to point the way to God and God's kingdom of compassion and justice.

Disciples witness to Jesus Christ in the world by following his teachings. They live his story by making his teachings, his life, his commandments part of their lives. This is how they live out their covenant relationship with God and God's church. Disciples bring good news to the poor, release the captives, open the eyes of the blind, and liberate the oppressed (Luke 4:16-18). They feed the hungry, give a drink to the thirsty, clothe the naked, welcome the homeless stranger, and visit the sick and the prisoners (Matthew 25:37-40). Disciples love God and love their neighbor as themselves (Matthew 22:34-40). They love one another as Christ loves them (John 13:34-35). They forgive as Christ forgives them (Matthew 18:21-22). In other words, disciples order their lives according to the teachings and commandments of their teacher, their Lord, their brother and friend: Jesus Christ. They do this so that the light of Christ may shine through them for the world, making them channels of grace.

A person is a channel of grace when he or she witnesses to Christ and follows his teachings. The General Rule of Discipleship, following Wesley's General Rules, suggests that Christ's life and teachings compel his disciples toward a balance between works of mercy (compassion and justice) and works of piety (worship and devotion). Within this balance between mercy and piety (loving God and loving neighbor) is an equal balance between social/public and personal/private acts that nurture the disciple's relationship with Christ.

Acts of compassion and devotion are those things that are done for one another. Acts of compassion are those things we do to meet the needs of the neighbor, who is anyone we encounter who is in need. "For I was hungry and you gave me food, I was thirsty and you gave me something to drink, I was a stranger and you welcomed me, I was naked and you gave me clothing, I was sick and you took care of me, I was in prison and you visited me" (Matthew 25:35-36).

Acts of devotion are those means of grace we practice in order to care for our personal relationship with God. Prayer, meditation, keeping a journal, fasting or abstinence serve to center our daily life in Christ. All personal relationships, if they are to grow and mature, require that the participants have regular time together to talk and listen to one another. The personal relationship with Christ is no different. If it is to grow and mature, it requires regular care and nurture. The means of grace are God's gift to the church by which God's children make themselves available to God and God's grace in Jesus Christ.

Acts of justice are related to acts of compassion, in that disciples ask the questions and take action to address the issues that are the cause of their neighbor's suffering. While compassion is the act of giving food to a hungry person, an act of justice addresses the institutional and structural issues that are the cause of the person's hunger. Justice is acting so that all people have what is needed to live and participate fully in the society in which they live (Deuteronomy 10:18; Psalm 10:18; Isaiah 58:1-12; 61:1-2; Jeremiah 5:28).

Finally, worship is the public giving of ourselves to God. It is what the gathered body of Christ does on Sunday morning. At the center of Christian worship is the Lord's Supper. At Christ's table the people are invited to come and remember who and whose they are. The following hymn-poem written by Charles Wesley powerfully expresses this idea:

> Come, sinners, to the gospel feast,
> let every soul be Jesus' guest.
> Ye need not one be left behind,
> for God hath bid all humankind.

> Do not begin to make excuse;
> ah! do not you his grace refuse;
> your worldly cares and pleasures leave,
> and take what Jesus hath to give.

> Come and partake the gospel feast,
> be saved from sin, in Jesus rest;
> O taste the goodness of our God,
> and eat his flesh and drink his blood.

> See him set forth before your eyes;
> behold the bleeding sacrifice;
> his offered love make haste to embrace,
> and freely now be saved by grace.

> Ye who believe his record true
> shall sup with him and he with you;
> come to the feast, be saved from sin,
> for Jesus waits to take you in.

Worship is the place Christians come to praise, sing, pray, hear the Word proclaimed, and give themselves to God and to one another. It is the public affirmation of faith in Christ and his grace. It is the work of the people through which sins are confessed and forgiveness is given and received. It is Christ's gift to the whole people of God. It is acting out in ritual the life to which disciples are called by Christ to live in the world.

The Holy Spirit guides and empowers disciples to be Christ's faithful witnesses in the world. Grace is present for all in the Holy Spirit that leads and equips Christ's disciples to live together as the church and to serve Christ in the world through acts of compassion, justice, worship, and devotion. John Wesley understood grace to be "the power of [God's] Holy Spirit, which alone worketh in us all that is acceptable in his sight." (From "The Good Steward," in *The Works of John Wesley,* Volume 2, edited by Albert C. Outler, page 286. © 1985 Abingdon Press. Used by permission.) He understood the Holy Spirit to be God's presence and power working in, through, and with disciples of Jesus to help them to be obedient to Christ's commands to love God with their whole heart, soul, mind, and strength, and to love their neighbor as themselves. Disciples have this power only by virtue of the Holy Spirit's working in and with them. For Wesley, discipleship is the work of the Holy Spirit in the daily lives of women and men, girls and boys who have responded affirmatively to God's grace offered to them in Jesus Christ.

The Holy Spirit gives disciples the assurance of forgiveness of sins and reconciliation with God and places within the human heart the desire to follow and serve Christ in the world. The Holy Spirit leads disciples to be obedient to Christ's commandments and empowers them to employ their gifts for ministry with and for Christ. Finally, the Holy Spirit inspires and leads disciples to be accountable to one another and to Christ.

Conclusion

Accountable Discipleship is how disciples of Jesus Christ live in God's household. It is the living of God's household rules in their daily lives. The rules of the household were summarized by Jesus when he was asked which was the greatest commandment. He told his questioner to love God and to "love your neighbor as yourself." These household rules have been restated in the United Methodist tradition in the General Rules (Do no harm, by avoiding evil. Do good. Employ the means of grace) and in the General Rule of Discipleship ("To witness to Jesus Christ in the world, and to follow his teachings through acts of compassion, justice, worship, and devotion, under the guidance of the Holy Spirit"). These household rules have been given to the members of the family as a gift, in order to help them grow and mature in faith. As they grow and mature in faith, their character is conformed to that of the head of the household, the Triune God: Father, Son, and Holy Spirit.

In the pages that follow, we will consider what it means to live in God's household, the household of grace. Living in and by grace is what Accountable Discipleship is all about.

For Reflection and Discussion

1. In the parable of the prodigal son, with which character do you most identify? Have you ever come home after a time of trial or alienation from loved ones? What did you experience on returning home?
2. Does your faith community feel like home to you? Who is the head of the household? What are the household rules?
3. Name some of the covenants in which you participate. How are they like God's covenant with you in baptism?

To Learn More

A Bishop's Reflections, by Kenneth L. Carder (Franklin, TN: Providence House Publishers, 1996).

Good News to the Poor: John Wesley's Evangelical Economics, by Theodore Jennings (Nashville: Abingdon Press, 1990).

Guide for Class Leaders: A Model for Christian Formation, by Grace Bradford (Nashville: Discipleship Resources, 1999).

Guide for Covenant Discipleship Groups, by Gayle Turner Watson (Nashville: Discipleship Resources, 2000).

Living Our Beliefs: The United Methodist Way, by Kenneth L. Carder (Nashville: Discipleship Resources, 1996).

Sprouts: Nurturing Children Through Covenant Discipleship, by Edie Genung Harris and Shirley L. Ramsey (Nashville: Discipleship Resources, 1995).

This Gift of Water: The Practice and Theology of Baptism Among Methodists in America, by Gayle Carlton Felton (Nashville: Abingdon Press, 1992).

Together in Love: Covenant Discipleship With Youth, by David C. Sutherland (Nashville: Discipleship Resources, 1999).

(Books from Discipleship Resources can be ordered through the online bookstore, http://www.discipleshipresources.org, or by phone, 800-685-4370.)

Chapter 2

The Foundation: Accountable Discipleship and the Bible

The Bible is the foundation of Accountable Discipleship. We begin with the Bible because that is where John Wesley began. He referred to himself as "a man of one book." That one book is the Bible. The Bible shaped his ministry of preaching, teaching, and organizing the people called Methodists. One of Wesley's most important and influential sermons is "The Scripture Way of Salvation." In it he shows, through the witness of Scripture, the saving power of grace revealed and offered to all the world in Jesus Christ.

> How plain and simple a thing...is the genuine religion of Jesus Christ! Provided only that we take it in its native form, just as it is described in the oracles of God. It is exactly suited by the wise Creator and Governor of the world to the weak understanding and narrow capacity of man in his present state. How observable is this both with regard to the end it proposes and the means to attain that end! The end is, in one word, salvation: the means to attain it, faith.
>
> (From "The Scripture Way of Salvation," in *The Works of John Wesley,* Volume 2, edited by Albert C. Outler, pages 155–56. © 1985 Abingdon Press. Used by permission.)

Here, Wesley contends that the message of salvation contained in the Scriptures may be understood and claimed by sinful, weak, imperfect human beings. The Word of God is such that it is accessible to all:

rich and poor, educated and uneducated, Christian and non-Christian, male and female. The Bible is God's story of salvation, within which is the story of the human response, individual and corporate, to God's saving work. The word used to name this human response to God's grace is *discipleship;* therefore, we begin our exploration of Accountable Discipleship at the beginning, the Bible.

The image I have chosen to describe the character and nature of discipleship is life in God's household. The Bible is filled with household language as it describes God's relationship with God's people. Having a home means having access to life. Home is where we receive all that is needed to live. Home is where we know we have a place at the table and will receive a share of all that is on it. Home is where we are accepted for who we are, as we are. We have access to life when we are part of a household. Homelessness is death. The God of the Bible is the God of life, the first homemaker.

The first and second chapters of Genesis tell the stories of God as creator of all that is needed for life and the establishment of home for God's people. Genesis 1:26-31 and Genesis 2:18-25 are stories of the creation of the first human family. In these stories we see that God relates to human beings through the basic unit of the family household.

In the twelfth chapter of Genesis, God chooses Abraham and Sarah (a family, a household), whom God blesses to be a blessing for the world. Because they trusted God and God's promise, Abraham and Sarah left their home and followed God to their new home, the new land God had promised them. Their faith in God's promise of an heir assured them that their life would continue into God's future. In the birth of their son Isaac the future of their household was assured.

The story of Joseph (Genesis 37–50) is the story of the descendants of Abraham moving from home in their own land (the land of their ancestor), to homelessness, and eventually to slavery in Egypt.

Exodus tells the story of God making a covenant with the Hebrew slaves in Egypt and delivering them to freedom. The Hebrew people were homeless foreigners. Because they were homeless, they were subject to death. God saw their misery, heard their cries, and knew their suffering (Exodus 3:7). Therefore, God, with the help of Moses and Aaron, brought them from homelessness to freedom and the promise of a land that would become their home, a land flowing with milk and honey. This Promised Land is home because in it they would be free. In addition to providing for their basic physical needs for food, water, and shelter, God gave the people the Law at Sinai. These were the household rules needed for the building of community. God the lawgiver is also God the homemaker.

The language of God's relationship with God's people is the language of household. God is called Father (Psalm 68:5; 89:26; 103:13; Isaiah 9:6; 63:16; 64:8; Jeremiah 3:19; 31:9; Malachi 1:6; Matthew 6:9; 28:19; Luke 11:2; 23:34; John 5:17; 14:2; Romans 8:15; Galatians 4:6; Revelation 3:5) and, on occasion, Mother (Isaiah 66:13). The people of Israel are God's children, members of God's household (Deuteronomy 14:1; Isaiah 29:23; 45:11; Jeremiah 3:14; Hosea 1:10; John 1:12; Romans 8:14-17; Galatians 3:26-28; Ephesians 1:5; 5:1-2; Philippians 2:15; 1 John 3:1-2). This is the language of familial relationship. It is the language of intimate, self-giving love. God is the loving parent who is head of the household, the one who provides for God's children. God gives of God's self to assure that everyone is known by name, is loved and accepted, has a place at the family table and shares in its bounty. God's love is covenant love, which is the love that creates home.

God's household is the center of compassion and justice for God's children. There are several dimensions to God's household. In its broadest sense, it encompasses the whole of creation. It is the world that God so loved that God gave God's own Son, "so that everyone who believes in him may not perish but may have eternal life" (John 3:16). (It is important to understand that eternal life is life with the Eternal One, God.) The earth, like God, brings forth and sustains life. God's children depend on the earth for water, air, and food. As members of God's family, they are given the responsibility of caring for and respecting the earth, so that it will provide for future generations.

God's household also is the whole of human community. All people are created by God and bear God's image within them (Genesis 1:27). God is like a loving parent for all of humankind. As members of God's household, each person is entitled to life, liberty, and love. In like manner, God's relationship with each person is characterized by compassion and justice, the defining spirit of covenant love.

Finally, God's household is the church, which is the covenant community given birth by Jesus Christ for the world. The household of the church is God's representative to the broader human community. It is the family called by God to be salt and light for the world (Matthew 5:13-16). In other words, the church is to be a sign community that points the way to God through its life, witness, and mission. That is why one of the apostle Paul's favorite names for the church is "the body of Christ" (Romans 7:4; 1 Corinthians 10:16; 12:27; Ephesians 4:12). The church is the community through and in which the Spirit of Christ carries on Christ's work of bringing good news to the poor, release to the captives, recovery of sight to the blind, and freedom to the oppressed (Luke 4:18-19).

The church is God's covenant community, the household that exists to reflect the light of Christ for all the world to see. It is a household with open doors through which all are invited and welcome without regard to race, gender, class, or creed. The church is the household of the living God that exists for the world.

Baptism is the door through which one enters the church. The waters of baptism are a sign of God's covenant with each member of the household. The waters wash us clean of the guilt of sin and give us new life in Christ. The old is washed away, and everything becomes new. God promises always to be for and with those who receive the waters; to love the baptized, even though God knows there will be times when they will feel unlovable; and to forgive and help the baptized repent when they struggle with sin in their lives. In other words, baptism is how a person becomes a member of God's household. In the waters of baptism, we are marked as God's own and adopted as God's daughters and sons, and as sisters and brothers to one another and to Jesus Christ.

> For all who are led by the Spirit of God are children of God. For you did not receive a spirit of slavery to fall back into fear, but you have received a spirit of adoption. When we cry, "Abba! Father!" it is that very Spirit bearing witness with our spirit that we are children of God, and if children, then heirs, heirs of God and joint heirs with Christ.
> (Romans 8:14-17a)

> But you are a chosen race, a royal priesthood, a holy nation, God's own people, in order that you may proclaim the mighty acts of him who called you out of darkness into his marvelous light.
> Once you were not a people,
>   but now you are God's people;
> once you had not received mercy,
>   but now you have received mercy.   (1 Peter 2:9-10)

Baptism is Christ's gift for all people who want to become members of God's household, the church. With this gift comes responsibility. The gift is free, and the acceptance and forgiveness are unconditional; but these gifts came at a high cost to the head of the household: the death of God's Son on the cross. Christ died so that all the world may live free from slavery to sin and the fear of death. He took all the sin of the world into himself and died our death (Romans 6:1-4). In his resurrection, Christ destroyed death's power to oppress humankind (1 Corinthians 15:54-58).

The life God gives in baptism is not the life the world gives (John 14:27); it is the life of Christ. Our part in the Baptismal Covenant is to "renounce the spiritual forces of wickedness, reject the evil powers of this world, and repent of [our] sin." Christ calls us to "accept the freedom and power God gives [us] to resist evil, injustice, and oppression in whatever forms they present themselves." And as God's children, we are to "confess Jesus Christ as [our] Savior, put [our] whole trust in his grace, and promise to serve him as [our] Lord, in union with the church which Christ has opened to people of all ages, nations, and races." (From "Baptismal Covenant I," in *The United Methodist Hymnal,* page 34. © 1976, 1980, 1985, 1989 The United Methodist Publishing House. Used by permission.)

The Baptismal Covenant is a covenant of grace, of responsible grace. The grace given and received is grace that invites response. How does one respond? How do children respond to the love of a faithful parent? They do the best they can to live lives pleasing to their mother and father. Children who are loved unconditionally, nurtured, and accepted for who they are generally respond to such love with joyful obedience. In the process they are formed into the image of their parents. They learn how to love and forgive as they have been loved and forgiven. This is the life offered to us in baptism. This is the life of faithful discipleship.

Granted, we hear reports every day in the news about parents who neglect and abuse their children. We are told that the family is broken. For those who come from a broken home or who were abused and neglected by a parent, the image of God as Father/Mother and Home-maker may be difficult to see. I pray that the image of God presented here helps them understand that abuse and neglect of children at the hands of parents is not God's will. God's heart grieves for the children who suffer at the hands that were intended to nurture and love them. I invite these people to see God the Father/Mother as the loving parent they never had. Jesus is the compassionate brother, their advocate and guide. The church, as God's household, then becomes the family where it is safe to be themselves. It is the place where they can count on being comforted, accepted, forgiven, and on being known by name. "But now thus says the LORD, he who created you…, he who formed you…: Do not fear, for I have redeemed you; I have called you by name, you are mine" (Isaiah 43:1).

Accountable Discipleship and the Law

Now this law is an incorruptible picture of the high and holy One that inhabiteth eternity. It is he whom in his essence no man hath seen or can see, made visible to men and angels. It is the face of God unveiled; God manifested to his creatures as they are able to bear it; manifested to give and not to destroy life; that they may see God and live. It is the heart of God disclosed to man.

(From "The Original, Nature, Properties, and Use of the Law," in *The Works of John Wesley,* Volume 2, edited by Albert C. Outler, page 9. © 1985 Abingdon Press. Used by permission.)

The Bible tells us how God wants God's children to live together in God's household (Exodus 20:1-17; Amos 5:24; Micah 6:8). Like most human households, God's household has rules. The purpose of the rules is to assure that everyone, including the head of the household, receives the respect he or she deserves. The household and each household member is guaranteed honor and regard for person and property. The household rules are intended to help everyone live together in peace, knowing that each member of the household is valued. In the Bible these household rules are known as the Law.

The Law is God's revealed will for human beings and human community. It is the covenant between God and humankind. The Law helps human beings know who they are and whose they are. It is God's way of describing God's relationship with the people of Israel and, through Israel, with all the world. In the Law, God also provides the basic rules for human conduct and relationships and the foundation on which human community may be established. The essence of the Law is found in the Ten Commandments given to Israel through Moses on Mount Sinai:

> Then God spoke all these words: I am the LORD your God, who brought you out of the land of Egypt, out of the house of slavery; you shall have no other gods before me.
>
> You shall not make for yourself an idol, whether in the form of anything that is in heaven above, or that is on the earth beneath, or that is in the water under the earth. You shall not bow down to them or worship them...
>
> You shall not make wrongful use of the name of the LORD your God, for the LORD will not acquit anyone who misuses his name.
>
> Remember the sabbath day, and keep it holy....
>
> Honor your father and your mother, so that your days may be long in the land that the LORD your God is giving you.
>
> You shall not murder.
>
> You shall not commit adultery.
>
> You shall not steal.
>
> You shall not bear false witness against your neighbor.
>
> You shall not covet your neighbor's house...or anything that belongs to your neighbor.   (Exodus 20:1-17)

The first three commandments describe the nature of God's relationship with God's people. This is the God who created them, the one who saw the misery and injustice of their slavery, heard their cries for deliverance, knew their suffering, and, by the power of God's own hand, set them free. This same God led them through the wilderness and made a covenant with them to be their God, shepherd, advocate, judge, healer, and comforter. God commands that, in response to this amazing grace, the people are to give their undivided loyalty to God. They are to forsake worship of any other gods, refrain from manufacturing any idols or images that would represent or limit God in any way, and to respect the name of God (use it only for good, never for evil).

The fourth commandment tells the people to honor God, the earth, and themselves by resting each seventh day. No work is to be done on the sabbath, for it is to be a day set aside not for doing but for being. The sabbath is God's day for re-creation of the body and the spirit. The sabbath is also a time for remembering. It is a day set aside by God for God's people to remember where they came from: They were once slaves in Egypt, but now they are free. God is their deliverer. Sabbath is a sacred time for God's children to recall their former life in bondage, to celebrate their present life in freedom, and to look forward to the promise of their new home in the land flowing with milk and honey.

The remaining six commandments describe how life in human community is to be ordered under God's rule and care. These commandments are a declaration of human rights that assure the members of the community safety for themselves and their property. They set the limits of life in community and are the rules by which God's children are to live in peace with one another.

The Law is important for Accountable Discipleship because in the commandments we see the balance between being and doing that is characteristic of the life of faith, and of Christian discipleship. For faith to be genuine and true, it must be balanced between being and doing. For example, disciples of Jesus need to take time to be with him, to pray and to listen. They need to listen for God's still small voice (1 Kings 19:12). Being attentive and available to God is possible only through the discipline of prayer and meditation. The first four commandments are given to help provide focus and space for being for and with God.

The second tablet of the commandments (You shall not murder, commit adultery, steal, lie, or covet) describes behaviors to avoid. Conversely, they shape the life of faith in the God of life. These commandments describe a life that is community oriented and, in all of its dimensions, sacred. This way of living regards the neighbor with dignity and respect. People of faith look to these commandments for direction on how they are to love their neighbor as they love themselves: protect life, be faithful to your spouse, be satisfied with what you have, tell the truth, share what you have with those who have less. Being and doing are the two sides of faith. The Law is God's gift to help God's children live balanced lives that are centered on loving God and their neighbors.

Unloading the Overload

The Law, with all its power and grace, is not where we find salvation. The Law leads, prompts, cajoles, and convinces us of our need for the salvation given to all the world in the life, death, and resurrection of Jesus Christ. In Romans 3:21-26, the apostle Paul describes what God has done to restore right relationship with the world:

> But now, apart from law, the righteousness of God has been disclosed, and is attested by the law and the prophets, the righteousness of God through faith in Jesus Christ for all who believe. For there is no distinction, since all have sinned and fall short of the glory of God; they are now justified by his grace as a gift, through the redemption that is in Christ Jesus, whom God put forward as a sacrifice of atonement by his blood, effective through faith. He did this to show his righteousness, because in his divine forbearance he had passed over the sins previously committed; it was to prove at the present time that he himself is righteous and that he justifies the one who has faith in Jesus.

In Romans 3:27, Paul says: "Then what becomes of boasting? It is excluded. By what law? By that of works? No, but by the law of faith. For we hold that a person is justified by faith apart from works prescribed by the law."

Paul assures us that all have sinned; all have fallen short of the righteousness of God. Nothing we can do could ever earn us God's acceptance or forgiveness, for we remain sinners no matter how scrupulously we keep the Law. The only one capable of reaching across the chasm created by sin is God, who comes to us in Jesus Christ. In the death and resurrection of Christ, God has destroyed sin's power to keep human beings alienated from their creator. In Christ, crucified and risen, God has restored the possibility of right relationship with God's creation. All this is God's initiative. It is what we call grace, a gift freely given to all who will accept it, trust in its power, and live by its ideals.

This belief in the forgiveness of sins and reconciliation with God through the life, death, and resurrection of Jesus Christ is known as the doctrine of justification, which is one of the core beliefs of the church. As Paul says, "For by grace you have been saved through faith, and this is not your own doing; it is the gift of God" (Ephesians 2:8). In other words, "God so loved the world that he gave his only Son, so that everyone who believes in him may not perish but may have eternal life. Indeed, God did not send the Son into the world to condemn the world, but in order that the world might be saved through him" (John 3:16-17). In Jesus Christ God's acceptance of the world, of every human being, is complete. We receive the gift of faith when we accept God's acceptance of us. It is entirely God's work in, for, and with us. It is a gift of grace.

Unfortunately, over the centuries the doctrine of justification by grace through faith has been overloaded on the side of faith. Fearing people would boast that they could earn their salvation by being good, some have dismissed the importance of the good works that are commanded by the Law. These people misunderstand Paul's seeming belief that Christ has replaced the Law, that somehow the Law is no longer needed because of what God has done in Christ. They teach and believe that all they need for faithful discipleship is faith and trust in God and in God's grace revealed in Jesus Christ. But a closer reading of the Gospels and of Paul's letters tells only part of the truth. "Do we then overthrow the law by this faith? By no means! On the contrary, we uphold the law" (Romans 3:31).

The problem with this overload is that it removes the Law entirely from the realm of Christian life. Good works become optional, things to be done when we feel like doing them. Discipleship is reduced to ascribing to a set of beliefs about God, Jesus Christ, and the Holy Spirit. Good works are suspect as "filthy cloth" (Isaiah 64:6). What is behind this overloaded doctrine is the commendable desire to discourage a works righteousness (the belief that being good, doing good works, and living a righteous life will earn God's acceptance). The overloaded doctrine of justification is a radical, albeit too radical, trust in the saving power of grace, which completely dismisses any human participation in salvation. To allow any human participation would be works righteousness.

John Wesley struggled with this very problem throughout most of his ministry. He sought to restore a proper balance to the doctrine of justification and believed that human beings are indeed saved by grace through faith. Wesley affirmed that no human effort or merit could earn God's acceptance. Salvation was entirely God's act in Christ, crucified and risen. Wesley also believed and taught that human beings participate in their own salvation, by accepting the gift of faith and the saving relationship with God in Jesus Christ by living their lives as the new creation (2 Corinthians 5:17). "For we are what he has made us, created in Christ Jesus for good works, which God prepared beforehand to be our way of life" (Ephesians 2:10). These good works are the result of promptings of the Holy Spirit to live lives faithful to the Law, which is the revealed will of God for human life and community. For Wesley, good works were not an optional part of Christian life and discipleship but a necessary means to "work out [our] own salvation" (Philippians 2:12).

Wesley believed that the Law had three functions: to convict, convert, and sustain the believer. He saw Romans 7:12 ("So the law is holy, and the commandment is holy and just and good") as affirmation from Paul that faith in Christ does not remove the believer from obedience to the Law.

> The law of God… is a copy of the eternal mind, a transcript of the divine nature; yea, it is the fairest offspring of the everlasting Father, the brightest efflux of his essential wisdom, the visible beauty of the Most High. It is the delight and wonder of cherubim and seraphim and all the company of heaven, and the glory and joy of every wise believer, every well instructed child of God upon earth.
>
> (From "The Original, Nature, Properties, and Use of the Law," in *The Works of John Wesley*, Volume 2, edited by Albert C. Outler, page 10. © 1985 Abingdon Press. Used by permission.)

> Now this law is an incorruptible picture of the high and holy One that inhabiteth eternity.… It is the face of God unveiled; God manifested to his creatures as they are able to bear it; manifested to give and not to destroy life; that they may see God and live. It is the heart of God disclosed to man.
>
> (From "The Original, Nature, Properties, and Use of the Law," in *The Works of John Wesley*, Volume 2, edited by Albert C. Outler, page 9. © 1985 Abingdon Press. Used by permission.)

In other words, for Wesley the Law is a reflection of Christ. Its purpose is to convict people of their sin and convince them of their need for God. As it convicts them of their sin, it draws them to Jesus Christ, the one who takes away sin, forgives, reconciles, and makes whole. Believers, once convicted and converted, are sustained by the Law in their new life in Christ by seeing in them God's will for them and the world. Wesley saw the Law not as something to be overcome but as grace that draws people to Christ and keeps them with him as their faith grows.

> Therefore I cannot spare the law one moment, no more than I can spare Christ; seeing I now want it as much to keep me to Christ as ever I wanted it to bring me to him. Otherwise this "evil heart of unbelief" would immediately "depart from the living God." Indeed each is continually sending me to the other—the law to Christ, and Christ to the law. On the one hand, the height and depth of the law constrain me to fly to the love of God in Christ; on the other, the love of God in Christ endears the law to me "above gold or precious stones"; seeing I know every part of it is a gracious promise, which my Lord will fulfill in its season.
>
> (From "The Original, Nature, Properties, and Use of the Law," in *The Works of John Wesley*, Volume 2, edited by Albert C. Outler, page 18. © 1985 Abingdon Press. Used by permission.)

Accountable Discipleship was Wesley's answer to the overloaded doctrine of justification. In it we find the necessary balance between faith and works. The grace of Christ saves and leads us to follow him and to do the good works for which we were created.

> What good is it, my brothers and sisters, if you say you have faith but do not have works? Can faith save you? If a brother or sister is naked and lacks daily food, and one of you says to them, "Go in peace; keep warm and eat your fill," and yet you do not supply their bodily needs, what is the good of that? So faith by itself, if it has no works, is dead.
> (James 2:14-17)

Accountable Discipleship helps Christians gain the balance between faith and works that leads to faithful discipleship and witness to Christ in the world. It empowers people to incorporate into their lives the commands of Christ to "love the Lord your God with all your heart, and with all your soul, and with all your mind" and to "love your neighbor as yourself" (Matthew 22:37, 39).

Scriptural Building Blocks

In the following pages, we will look at five biblical passages (Micah 6:6-8; John 15:1-17; Matthew 22:34-40; Matthew 25:31-46; Philippians 2:5-13) that demonstrate the balance between faith and works, being and doing, which is a hallmark of faithful discipleship. They illustrate the disciple's need to follow Christ and his way of living in the world through acts of compassion, justice, worship, and devotion. The Scriptures reveal to us the truth that discipleship is possible only by grace, and that the good works we are called to do are means of grace. This is to say that they are ways through which grace is conveyed by God and experienced by the disciples. If disciples fail to incorporate them into their lives, they run the risk of excluding themselves from the saving, healing grace of Christ.

These passages are by no means exhaustive, for there are many others. These were chosen because each addresses the need for a healthy balance between faith and works as people come to faith and seek to follow, love, and obey Jesus and his commandments.

What Does the Lord Require? (Micah 6:6-8)

"With what shall I come before the LORD,
  and bow myself before God on high?
Shall I come before him with burnt offerings,
  with calves a year old?

Will the LORD be pleased with thousands of rams,
    with ten thousands of rivers of oil?
Shall I give my firstborn for my transgression,
    the fruit of my body for the sin of my soul?"
He has told you, O mortal, what is good;
    and what does the LORD require of you
but to do justice, and to love kindness,
    and to walk humbly with your God?

                        (Micah 6:6-8)

Micah describes the relationship between humankind and God. He is keenly aware of human weakness and sin because he witnessed how poor, vulnerable, and voiceless people were systematically exploited and oppressed by the rich and powerful. He observed the abuse of power and the corrupting influence of wealth. Micah's ministry was that of a prophet, who was called by God to speak God's word of justice and righteousness to the king and his court. Micah's message, like that of most prophets, caused discomfort for the powerful and comfort for the powerless. He gave a word of warning, accompanied by God's promise for a future for God's people.

When we look at Micah 6:6-8, we see a description of the relationship between God and humankind. The story of this relationship is characterized as good news–bad news–good news.

The good news is that God is the creator of all that was, all that is, and all that ever will be. This same God who creates is a God of love, a God who loves all that God has created. According to the Scriptures, God has a special, abiding love for humankind. In fact, this God seeks a loving, intimate relationship with the entire human race, with each individual man, woman, and child. This relationship is characterized by a covenant initiated by God for the building up of God's people. This is good news because this covenant love provides one of the essential needs for human life: a home. God supplies all that is needed for human life and community to thrive and flourish: food, water, clothing, shelter, acceptance, love, and a rule of life (the Law) that teaches and guides the community toward righteousness and justice. God's love for the world is good news.

The bad news is that humankind has messed things up rather badly. We have rebelled against God and God's Law. We have turned our back on God's rule of life and sought our own rule, all to disastrous effect. Sin soon entered the picture, and with it came alienation from God and from one another, greed, jealousy, lust, violence, and hatred of all that is good. This sinfulness caused humans to love themselves more than they love God. We lived according to our own desires and brought death on ourselves and our world. When we realized what we had done, we recognized that nothing we could do, no amount of repentance or good works, could ever restore the relationship with God. It was as if a huge gulf existed between God and humankind. And there were no human arms long enough and no human effort great enough to bridge the chasm that separated us from the God who created us.

Fortunately, that is not the end of the story. In spite of the bad news caused by sin, there is more good news: God made a way. God reached with God's own arms across the chasm, which was caused by our disobedience and lust, to restore and mend the broken relationship. For Micah, this way was the Law. Christians, on the other hand, understand Jesus Christ to be God's redeeming and restoring way over the chasm. In other words, God has acted and done what humankind could never do. In the life, death, and resurrection of Jesus Christ, the incarnation of the Law (Matthew 5:17; John 14:6), God has forgiven the sins of humankind and made a way for the relationship to be restored and for human beings to be healed and made whole.

This good news–bad news–good news relationship is contained in Micah 6:6-8. Verses 6-7 describe how humankind, particularly the people of Judah, took the good news of God's covenant love for granted and turned away to live in sin. They oppressed the poor, neglected the widows and orphans, and mistreated the foreigners within their gates. And they wondered how to restore their broken relationship with God. Their way was to make sacrifices to God. Given the incredible quantities ("thousands of rams"), volumes ("ten thousands of rivers of oil"), and awfulness ("my firstborn") of the sacrifices, the people certainly were aware of the magnitude of their sins. The prophet understood that nothing and no human effort or sacrifice could ever restore a right relationship with a righteous and just God.

But then the prophet speaks for God and reminds the people that God has made a way for them (verse 8). God has made the initiative to restore the relationship and, by grace, will help the people live into that relationship. All that is required is for the people to repent, to turn away from their sin, oppression, injustice, and wickedness, and to turn toward God and God's way (the Law, the household rules).

The same applies to disciples of Jesus Christ. When they repent of their sins and turn toward God, they accept the gift of forgiveness and restored relationship with God. Their way of life then must be centered in Christ and no longer in themselves.

He has told you, O mortal, what is good;
  and what does the LORD require of you
but to do justice, and to love kindness,
  and to walk humbly with your God?
                                    (Micah 6:8)

The disciple's way of life is grounded in obedience to Christ's way of life. In that life there is an essential balance between doing ("to do justice…and to love kindness") and being ("walk humbly with your God"). This is to say that disciples of Jesus Christ are compassionate and just. They love their neighbor and their world through intentional, concrete actions. They love in word and deed, seeking the welfare of the least, the last, and the lost. Disciples are humble and practice humility in all that they do and speak. They do not think of themselves as being better or above anyone. Humility enables the disciples to see Christ in the face of each person they encounter in their daily lives. This humility arises out of their daily walk with God in prayer and meditation.

In Micah 6:6-8, we find a scriptural description of the life of discipleship. It is a life that is balanced between doing and being. Micah reminds disciples that they are sinful, fallible human beings who need the forgiveness and grace of God. He also reminds them that they are children of God and members of God's household. As members of the household, disciples have responsibilities to God and to their sisters and brothers to "do justice, and to love kindness, and to walk humbly with [their] God."

Bearing Fruit (John 15:1-17)

I am the true vine, and my Father is the vinegrower. He removes every branch in me that bears no fruit. Every branch that bears fruit he prunes to make it bear more fruit. You have already been cleansed by the word that I have spoken to you. Abide in me as I abide in you. Just as the branch cannot bear fruit by itself unless it abides in the vine, neither can you unless you abide in me. I am the vine, you are the branches. Those who abide in me and I in them bear much fruit, because apart from me you can do nothing. Whoever does not abide in me is thrown away like a branch and withers; such branches are gathered, thrown into the fire, and burned.   (John 15:1-6)

The vineyard is an image that is used often by biblical writers to describe God's household (Isaiah 5:1-7; 27:2-5; Jeremiah 12:10; Matthew 20:1-16). God's household is a source of life and hope for the community and a garden that requires much care before it bears fruit. It is no surprise, then, that biblical writers would use the vineyard to illustrate the nature of God's relationship with God's people.

In John 15:1-17, Jesus speaks of himself as the vine and God the Father as the gardener who tends and cares for the vineyard. As the vine, Jesus supplies the nourishment the branches need to live. The branches are his disciples, the people he has chosen and called to follow him (John 15:16). These branches, some of which are grafted into the vine, grow from the vine. The vine gives them the water and nutrients needed to bear fruit. When a branch fails to bear fruit over time, the gardener removes it to make room for new branches.

This is the last of Jesus' "I am" sayings in John. Jesus paints a picture of a community, in the image of the vine, that is characterized by interdependence and mutuality. If you have seen a grapevine, you know what Jesus is talking about. A grapevine is a jumble of branches that are twisted and turned with one another, making it difficult to know where one branch begins and another ends. Sometimes it is equally difficult to tell the vine from the branches.

The gardener, known as a vinedresser, tends the vine and branches. He or she cultivates the earth around the vine. An important job is that of pruning in the spring and fall, when the vinedresser cuts away branches that have not produced fruit. Those that bear fruit are trimmed back to help them produce more and better fruit. Pruning improves the likelihood that the vine will continue to grow and increase its yield. It also improves the quality of the fruit produced. Tending grapes is hard work that requires skill and patience. It is a work of love—love for the earth, the vine, the branches, and the good fruit.

As Jesus says in verse 1, God is like the vinedresser who loves the vineyard. God gives God's self to tenderly help the vine bear fruit (love). The branches (disciples) are given all they need to do the works of love that the vine (Christ) equips them to do. Those disciples who are faithful to the commands of Christ bear fruit through living lives of compassion and justice in the world. Worship and prayer are like breathing and eating to them, and loving God and their neighbor is part of their nature. These are the ones God prunes to help them bear more fruit. The pruning is grace working in their lives to remove any blockages that prevent them from doing more works of love for God and their neighbor.

On the other hand, God removes those branches that do not bear fruit. After a few seasons of pruning and cultivating, some branches simply refuse to bear fruit. These are the disciples who neglect their relationship with Christ and their neighbor. For a multitude of reasons, they stop listening to Christ. They disregard his commandments and ignore the need to do the works of love Christ requires of them. These are the ones God removes, or they remove themselves from the community. Once removed, they become subjects for renewed evangelical attention. The fire (15:6) is a cleansing fire that breaks down resistance and makes a way for repentance.

John Wesley used John 15:1-17 to support his arguments in opposition to the doctrines of predestination and the perseverance of the saints. He saw in this passage the need for living as a responsible participant in the life of Jesus Christ. The household is open to all who respond to grace and allow grace to flow through them for others. It is not limited to the elect, as the doctrine of predestination would lead Christians to believe. And membership in the household does not come without responsibility, as the doctrine of the perseverance of the saints conveys. The branches have a responsibility to bear fruit. When they bear fruit, they are pruned so they may bear more fruit. When they no longer bear fruit and do not respond to pruning, they are removed. This is, for Wesley, the function of accountability in the life of discipleship.

John 15:1-17 demonstrates that the grace given to the world in Christ is a responsible grace. This means that the grace Christ gives requires a response from those who receive it. It is freely offered and given, but those who accept and receive it must allow it to flow through them to bear fruit for God. This text also demonstrates that people do not live as disciples in isolation. Discipleship is lived in community like the vine and branches. The disciple is one who is chosen and called by Christ and, in baptism, is grafted into the vine. Disciples, like branches, depend on the vine and on one another to bear fruit. John 15 shows that discipleship is not a private, individualistic enterprise; it is life in community, for the world and for Christ.

Jesus said, "As the Father has loved me, so I have loved you; abide in my love. If you keep my commandments, you will abide in my love, just as I have kept my Father's commandments and abide in his love. I have said these things to you so that my joy may be in you, and that your joy may be complete" (John 15:9-11). Jesus welcomes his disciples into his household and life and loves them unconditionally. When his disciples accept and live in his love, he requires that his love become their way of life. His love is their new home; they abide in his love. The way to live in Christ's love is to order their lives according to his commandments to love God and neighbor. Disciples are accountable to Christ and to one another. As they grow in love and grace, they bear fruit for God, which is more love. Accountability is intended to help disciples live the life to which they have been called and bear fruit for the One who called them and who calls them friend.

The Great Commandment (Matthew 22:34-40)

> When the Pharisees heard that [Jesus] had silenced the Sadducees, they gathered together, and one of them, a lawyer, asked him a question to test him. "Teacher, which commandment in the law is the greatest?" He said to him, "'You shall love the Lord your God with all your heart, and with all your soul, and with all your mind.' This is the greatest and first commandment. And a second is like it: 'You shall love your neighbor as yourself.' On these two commandments hang all the law and the prophets." (Matthew 22:34-40)

Here, Jesus is being tested by the religious authorities when a scribe steps forward to ask him which of the commandments he thinks is the greatest. Jesus quotes Deuteronomy 6:4-5 and Leviticus 19:18 and gives a summary of the Decalogue (the Ten Commandments) as a guide for faithful discipleship. Jesus says that the greatest commandment is that which encompasses all of the commandments. The essence of the Law is love of God and love of neighbor and self. The whole of God's good news for the world is wrapped up in these commands to love.

What kind of love? A complete love and loyalty to God. The first commandment is a call to love God with the whole self. No part of human life and experience is exempt from God's love and our love for God. This is because God is the creator of all that we are and all that we have. Therefore, all that we are and all that we have belongs to God and is rightly used in accord with God's will. What is God's will but to love wholeheartedly? It is "to do justice, and to love kindness, and to walk humbly with [our] God" (Micah 6:8). Jesus is saying here that God's whole being is love, a self-giving, unconditional love that gives and sustains life.

This love for God is lived out in love for the neighbor. The way we live out this holistic love is through loving the neighbor as we love ourselves. In other words, the way we relate to our neighbor is to be a reflection of our relationship with God. If we love God, we must love our neighbor. And to love the neighbor is to act with compassion and justice. The love for God is to be a reflection of God's love, which is understood in the Scriptures as compassion and justice. This love is not self-centered. It is self-giving, abundant, generous, and just.

Finally, commandments are not optional activities. They come from God to give order to our life with God and our neighbor. Love is the order of God's household. If we wish to live in God's house as God's children, we must do our best to live by God's rule of love. Loving God, neighbor, and self is the responsibility of those who want to live under God's roof. Simply put, God expects us to love what God loves. This is why we love our neighbor as we love ourselves.

Household Living Is Serving (Matthew 25:31-46)

> "Come, you that are blessed by my Father, inherit the kingdom prepared for you from the foundation of the world; for I was hungry and you gave me food, I was thirsty and you gave me something to drink, I was a stranger and you welcomed me, I was naked and you gave me clothing, I was sick and you took care of me, I was in prison and you visited me." Then the righteous will answer him, "Lord, when was it that we saw you hungry and gave you food, or thirsty and gave you something to drink? And when was it that we saw you a stranger and welcomed you, or naked and gave you clothing? And when was it that we saw you sick or in prison and visited you?" And the king will answer them, "Truly I tell you, just as you did it to one of the least of these who are members of my family, you did it to me."   (Matthew 25:34-40)

In the parable of the judgment of the nations, Jesus teaches that members of God's household care for one another. Most of all, they care for the ones who are weak and vulnerable. Living in God's house means living a way of life characterized by compassion and justice for all people, especially the hungry, thirsty, naked, unwelcome, sick, and imprisoned ones whom the rest of the world has discarded and rendered as outcasts. These are the ones with whom God identifies.

Jesus clearly teaches that when we look into the faces of the homeless, the prisoner, the refugee, the AIDS patient, the death-row inmate, we are looking into his face. When members of God's household look beyond their own personal comfort and privilege and reach out with compassion to the neighbor, they are serving Christ himself and "[working] out [their] own salvation" (Philippians 2:12).

This parable helps us understand who our neighbor is. When Jesus commands his sisters and brothers, "You shall love your neighbor as yourself," he means that the neighbor is more than the people who live in your hometown, members of your church, or even citizens of the state in which you live. The neighbor is not just people who look like you. In Matthew 25:31-46, Jesus tells us that our neighbor is anyone who is in need. Moreover, when we reach out with compassion and justice to the neighbor, we are serving Christ himself.

Conversely, this parable tells us that neglect of the neighbor will lead to "eternal punishment" (Matthew 25:45-46). Abandoning the poor has eternal consequences. Refusing to come to the aid of the hungry when we have the means to give them the food they need separates us from Christ. When we walk away from the poor, we walk away from Christ. If we turn our back on the poor long enough and consistently enough, we eventually exclude ourselves from the household of God.

In Matthew 25:31-46, Christ tells his disciples how to love their neighbor. The love he teaches is a love that is self-giving and is characterized by compassion and justice. Loving and serving Christ means loving and serving the neighbor, anyone who is hungry, thirsty, outcast, naked, sick, or imprisoned. When we reach out with food to the hungry and clean water for the thirsty, open our door to the stranger, and visit the sick and the prisoner, we are serving Christ (Isaiah 58:6-12).

Having the Mind of Christ (Philippians 2:5-13)

Let the same mind be in you that was in Christ Jesus,
who, though he was in the form of God,
did not regard equality with God
as something to be exploited,
but emptied himself,
taking the form of a slave,
being born in human likeness.
And being found in human form,
he humbled himself
and became obedient to the
point of death—
even death on a cross.

Therefore God also highly
exalted him
and gave him the name
that is above every name,
so that at the name of Jesus
every knee should bend,
in heaven and on earth and
under the earth,
and every tongue should confess
that Jesus Christ is Lord,
to the glory of God the Father.

Therefore, my beloved, just as you have always obeyed me, not only in my presence, but much more now in my absence, work out your own salvation with fear and trembling; for it is God who is at work in you, enabling you both to will and to work for his good pleasure.
(Philippians 2:5-13)

Here, the apostle Paul teaches us that Christ is the model for discipleship. This ancient Christian hymn paints the picture of humility, obedience, and self-giving love that is the life of Christ for the world. Those who wish to follow Christ are invited to join him in this life of humble service, even to the point of suffering and death.

Paul tells us that discipleship is seeking the mind of Christ. How does one seek the mind of Christ? How does one have the mind of Christ? The mind of Christ comes as a result of living the life of Christ. To share in his mind, his truth, we need to look at his life and ministry. In his life we find balance between being and doing.

Because Jesus was an observant Jew, prayer, fasting, Scripture, and worship were central to his life. He understood the importance of having regular time alone with God and with himself. He knew the Scriptures well enough to be familiar with the fine points of the law and the prophets and to engage in theological reflection with his disciples and with the rabbis, scribes, and Pharisees. Jesus observed the sabbath and participated in the worship life of the synagogue and temple in Jerusalem. Because his task on earth was so great, it was necessary for Jesus to practice a rich devotional and worship life.

Jesus humbled himself and lived his life as a rabbi among the poor and dispossessed. He ate with sinners, prostitutes, tax collectors, and lepers. He healed the sick, opened the eyes of the blind, and cast out demons. Jesus traveled the countryside and villages preaching and teaching wherever he found people who would listen to him. He brought the good news of God's reign of justice and righteousness to the poor and the poor in spirit. "And being found in human form, he humbled himself and became obedient to the point of death—even death on a cross" (Philippians 2:8).

In Philippians 2:1-8, Paul describes who Christ is and the life he lived. In verses 12-13, he tells those who would follow this Christ: "Work out your own salvation with fear and trembling; for it is God who is at work in you, enabling you both to will and to work for his good pleasure." He is telling us that disciples of Jesus Christ need to imitate their Savior.

Discipleship is the living out of Christ's life in our own lives. It is looking at Christ, keeping our eyes on him, learning from him, and doing our best to imitate him. In other words, disciples are people who do the things Jesus did. They put into practice the things Jesus taught. They pray, fast, and worship the God of Abraham, Isaac, and Jacob. Disciples identify themselves with the poor, the weak, the strangers, the dispossessed, and the despised ones of the world. They bring good news to the poor, healing to the sick, and liberation to the imprisoned.

Disciples are people who "work out [their] own salvation" by following and participating in the life and ministry of Jesus Christ in the world. They do not work out their salvation alone, for they do it the way Jesus taught: within a community of mutual support and accountability. Just as Jesus needed the community of disciples to do his saving work, disciples throughout the ages have needed the love and support of Christian community to be faithful to Jesus. "For it is God who is at work in you, enabling you both to will and to work for [God's] good pleasure" (Philippians 2:13). It is God working through the community, enabling all members, all disciples, to live lives of justice, compassion, worship, and devotion. Grace flows through the community, the church, to empower disciples to live out their Baptismal Covenant. It is God, working by grace through the people, that gives disciples all they need to love God and love their neighbor as themselves.

The mind of Christ comes through living the life of Christ in the world. The General Rule of Discipleship is a means for living his life and learning his mind. As acts of compassion, justice, worship, and devotion are incorporated into our lives, we learn Christ's mind together in community. Imitating (living) his life opens us to the possibilities and power of grace. Grace flows through our lives for the world. In the process, the mind of Christ becomes our mind, our way of being and acting.

Conclusion

The Bible is the foundation for Accountable Discipleship. We find in the Scriptures the story of God's amazing grace at work in and for the world. This grace has come for humankind in the Jew from Galilee named Jesus. In his life we find the model for our lives and the means we need to become channels of grace for the world.

The foundation of a house is important because it is what holds everything up. We need a firm foundation in order for the house to stand and give us shelter. In the Bible God has given us the rules for living in God's household. John Wesley understood this; therefore, everything he did and taught was grounded in Scripture. His teaching and practice of discipleship is summarized in, among others, Galatians 5:6b: "The only thing that counts is faith working through love."

The Bible tells us the story of life in God's household as faith working through love. Here, we see the needed balance between being (faith) and doing (love). Faith is a gift from God, but it is not a static possession. Faith is a relationship with the living God, who has come to humankind in Jesus Christ. This relationship is dynamic and liberating. It sets us free from self-centeredness and for love. It turns us away from ourselves and toward Christ. This faith awakens the heart to God's love for me and for the world. It has meaning and power only when it is worked out in the world through love, the unconditional, justice-seeking, self-giving love of Jesus Christ.

For Reflection and Discussion

1. What did John Wesley mean when he referred to himself as "a man of one book"?
2. The Bible uses household and family language when describing the relationship between God and humankind. How is God Father and Mother for you? How is Jesus a brother for you?
3. What were the household rules you grew up with? Look at the Ten Commandments (Exodus 20:1-17) and describe some of the rules for living in God's household.
4. What is your understanding of God's household? Is it the church? the world? creation? the universe?
5. What is the relationship between the Law and grace?
6. What is the doctrine of justification? What does it have to do with discipleship?
7. Look at Romans 3:21-28 and James 2:14-26. What is the relationship between faith and works? Why is accountability needed?
8. Why is finding a balance between doing and being so important for the life of a disciple?
9. List some other Scripture passages that you think are important to understanding discipleship. Some may be Ephesians 2:1-10; James 2:14-26; 1 John 3:16-18.

To Learn More

Engaging the Powers: Discernment and Resistance in a World of Domination, by Walter Wink (Minneapolis: Fortress Press, 1992).

God the Economist: The Doctrine of God and Political Economy, by M. Douglas Meeks (Minneapolis: Fortress Press, 1989).

Let Justice Roll Down: The Old Testament, Ethics, and Christian Life, by Bruce C. Birch (Louisville: Westminster John Knox Press, 1991).

Living Toward a Vision: Biblical Reflections on Shalom, by Walter Brueggemann (New York: United Church Press, 1982).

Shaped by the Word: The Power of Scripture in Spiritual Formation, by M. Robert Mulholland, Jr. (Nashville: Upper Room Books, 1985).

The Prophetic Imagination, by Walter Brueggemann (Minneapolis: Fortress Press, 1978).

The Framework: A Theology for Accountable Discipleship

If the Bible is the foundation of discipleship, then theology is the framework that supports it. Theology is nothing more or less than thinking, talking, and writing about God. It is how we human beings try to understand who God is and how God is working in the world and in our lives. Doing theology is important because it helps us know who God is, who our neighbor is, and who we are. It is the exploration of the divine-human relationship. The more we understand who God is, the more we are able to understand ourselves and our place in the world. Theology is our way of making sense out of the life we have been given and how we are going to live it out on planet Earth.

It is unfortunate that in today's world theology has been perceived as belonging to the professionals, the academics and the clergy. Because of this perception, theology has become suspect by ordinary people. Many ordinary, faithful Christians have been convinced that theology is beyond their understanding, that only learned people are qualified to do it. Contributing to this unfortunate state of affairs is the lack of Bible reading and study among most people in the mainline churches, including The United Methodist Church. Consequently, the incredibly important task of doing theology has been surrendered to the academy. This means that doing theology has almost disappeared from the life of most local churches.

Doing theology is far too important to be left solely to the professional theologians. Most of them would agree. The recent growing interest and participation in serious Bible study (such as DISCIPLE) has led the way in helping ordinary people reclaim their role as theologians. As people study the Bible together, they naturally ask questions and wrestle with who God is and who they are in relation to God and their neighbor. Any time we think, ask questions, and talk about God in a thoughtful way grounded in Scripture, we are doing theology. Theology is how we understand who God is and who we are. Being a disciple of Jesus Christ also means being a theologian.

John Wesley and the Methodists understood this. Wesley was a practical theologian, in the sense that he sought to bring the good news of God in Jesus Christ to ordinary, practical people. On April 2, 1739, at the invitation of his friend George Whitefield, Wesley began open-air preaching. He wrote in his journal:

> At four in the afternoon I submitted to "be more vile," and proclaimed in the highways the glad tidings of salvation, speaking from a little eminence in a ground adjoining to the city, to about three thousand people. The Scripture on which I spoke was this (is it possible anyone should be ignorant that it is fulfilled in every true minister of Christ?): "The Spirit of the Lord is upon me, because he hath anointed me to preach the gospel to the poor. He hath sent me to heal the broken-hearted, to preach deliverance to the captives and recovery of sight to the blind, to set at liberty them that are bruised, to proclaim the acceptable year of the Lord."
>
> (From *The Works of John Wesley*, Volume 19, edited by W. Reginald Ward and Richard P. Heitzenrater, page 46. © 1990 Abingdon Press. Used by permission.)

Wesley saw that the church of his day, the Church of England, was doing little to reach the ordinary people with the gospel of Jesus Christ. As a priest of the church, he believed that the only appropriate place for preaching was in the sanctified confines of a church building. But the unfortunate reality of eighteenth-century England was that few people, rich or poor, attended the church's services of worship. Many of the priests had become cynical and lazy and did not care for the people. The preaching and worship of the church said little to the everyday reality of the people's lives. It left a void that was filled by a number of religious societies and dynamic preachers, such as Whitefield and Wesley. The people were hungry for God, and they needed to hear and receive the good news of God's grace offered to them in the person of Jesus Christ. Rather than wait and hope that the people would come to him, Wesley parted with church tradition and "submitted to be more vile." In other words, he moved from the confines of the church sanctuary to the fields and squares where the common people were. Wesley took the good news of Christ to the people.

Wesley was a practical theologian because of how he did theology and with whom he did it. He met people where they were and did not speak down to them but spoke in words and in a way they could understand. Just as important as how he did theology is the people with whom and for whom he did it: the poor and working people of his day. Wesley chose to go to the ordinary people on whose backs the British Empire was built. In that sense, Wesley walked in Jesus' footsteps. It is no surprise, then, that the text for his first open-air sermon was Luke 4:18: "The Spirit of the Lord is upon me, because he has anointed me to bring good news to the poor. He has sent me to proclaim release to the captives and recovery of sight to the blind, to let the oppressed go free." Practical theology is theology that speaks from and with the people among whom Jesus lived and taught: the poor, the captives, the blind, and the oppressed. This is where Methodist theology, the theology of Accountable Discipleship, begins and ends.

The Wesleyan approach to doing theology is practical because it employs four essential elements that build on, inform, and interpret one another: Scripture, tradition, experience, and reason. We will look at each of these in the order of their weight.

Scripture

The Bible is the starting point for all theology and, most particularly, for Wesleyan theology. In Chapter 2, we established the essential nature of Scripture to John Wesley. For him, Scripture was the foundation on which all his faith and work were built. It was the filter through which everything must pass before it could be deemed acceptable and faithful to Christ. Wesley believed and taught that the Bible was God's word, a gift of God's self to and for the world. It contained all that was needed for people to learn and practice holiness of heart and life. In the Scriptures, those who sought God could find him.

Scripture is the first and most important of the four elements of Wesleyan theology. In other words, tradition, experience, and reason must be built on the foundation of Scripture. They each must be supported by the Word of God if they are to be regarded as faithful and true to Christ.

Wesley believed that Scripture has primacy because it is the revealed word of God for the people of God. It is God's story from which all human tradition, experience, and reason must flow.

Another way of looking at this is that Scripture is like a prism. When light passes through a prism, it is separated into its various component colors: red, orange, yellow, green, blue, indigo, and violet. We can know if our traditions, experience, and reason are faithful to Scripture and to the Spirit of Christ when they are some shade of the colors contained in the light of Christ that passes through its prism. Those traditions, experiences, and ideas that do not align with or will not pass through the prism of Scripture are not of God. They either need to be corrected or cast aside. It is important for us to understand that each color of the rainbow has many shades, permitting and validating the many and varied traditions, experiences, and ideas that can be found within the universal church of Jesus Christ. Christ does not require that all be the same shade of red or blue; however, they need to be within the spectrum. Scripture, therefore, is a gift from God to help us know God's story and find our story in God's story. It also helps us discern the things of God from those that pretend to be of God. This is why Wesley affirmed the primacy of Scripture in all matters of faith and life.

Tradition

Tradition is the combined experiences, beliefs, and practices of the community that are passed down from generation to generation. Many of the central traditions of the church, such as baptism and the Lord's Supper, have their origin in Scripture. They have been handed down as means of remembering who God is and who we are as people of God. When we participate in the traditions, we remember that we are children of God and sisters and brothers of one another. We belong to the God who created and is forming us into the image of Christ. The Scriptures and tradition tell us that, as children of God, we are welcome and have a place at God's table. Tradition connects us to the past, to our ancestors in the faith who lived and died in Christ (Hebrews 12:1). As we are joined to the faithful ones of the past, we are more able to walk faithfully into the future with confidence in who we are as sisters and brothers in Christ and as children of God.

Wesley placed great value on the tradition of the church. He studied the writings of the early church fathers and mothers and drank at the well of their wisdom and experience in living out their faith. Wesley believed that participation in the traditions of baptism, the Lord's Supper, prayer, small groups, and fasting were means of grace. These traditions were ways of connecting with God and God's amazing grace. He believed that the traditions helped people receive and allow God's grace to flow through them. Making these traditions, these means of grace, part of daily life were, for Wesley and the Methodists, part of being a disciple of Jesus Christ in the world.

Experience

Wesley also placed great value on human experience as a way of knowing God and understanding self. In fact, for Wesley, experience sometimes took precedence over tradition. For example, his decision to begin open-air preaching was a significant departure from tradition for him. Wesley agreed with the teaching of the church that the only appropriate place for proclaiming the Holy Word of God was within the consecrated confines of the church. It did not matter if anyone was there to hear the Word. What mattered, according to tradition, was that if the Word was to be proclaimed, it must be preached from a pulpit in a church building. This caused conflict within Wesley when he heard of and finally witnessed the great crowds of people who went to hear George Whitefield preach in the fields outside Bristol. He saw churches where few people actually entered, especially the working, poor, and ordinary people. He saw George Whitefield breaking with tradition and reaching thousands of people a day with the good news of Christ. When Whitefield decided to go help with the growing revival in America and invited Wesley to continue his ministry in Bristol, Wesley felt much ambivalence. At first Wesley knew he could not do it because field preaching was discouraged in many quarters of the church. But his experience of the people and the potential for ministry caused him to reevaluate the tradition. After much struggle, searching the Scriptures, and prayer, Wesley accepted Whitefield's invitation, and an important chapter of the Methodist movement was begun.

Wesley believed that God speaks to us through our day-to-day experiences of life and the world around us. Therefore, he encouraged the practice of the means of grace—the public worship of God, personal and family prayer, the Lord' Supper, studying and meditating with Scripture, participating in a small group for support and accountability (otherwise known as Christian conferencing), and fasting—as ways of being open to experiencing God to bring transformation and healing. Wesley referred to these as the instituted means of grace. These practices, when incorporated into daily life, enable Christians to experience God regularly. They open the heart and mind to be more available to God so that grace can flow through their lives.

In addition to the instituted means of grace, Wesley also encouraged practices known as prudential means of grace. These are the opportunities God provides for people to be channels and receivers of grace as they go about their daily lives. A good place to find a description of these means of grace is Matthew 25:31-40. In this parable, Jesus tells his disciples that feeding the hungry, giving a drink to the thirsty, clothing the naked, welcoming the stranger, and visiting the sick and imprisoned are important for spiritual well-being. In other words, when a disciple sees hungry people and takes the time to give them something to eat, the disciple is both a channel and a recipient of grace. The act of serving people who are suffering or in need is a means of grace. According to the parable, it also is serving Christ himself. The prudential means of grace help disciples experience Christ in the world. Wesley believed that such experiences went hand in hand with tradition and the Scriptures.

Reason

The final element of Wesley's practical theological method was reason. While he often is quoted as being "a man of one book" (the Bible), Wesley was a voracious reader. He read and studied everything from theology to the sciences. He was a man of the Enlightenment, which means that Wesley understood the importance of empirical knowledge (understanding gained by practical experience, not by theory or speculation). Wesley possessed a keen mind for reasoning, which he used with both his supporters and opponents. He also believed that reason was another means by which God is revealed to humankind, and that it is a means for helping humans know God and ourselves.

Reason is important as a way for believing and living as a disciple because of the first and greatest commandment: "You shall love the Lord your God with all your heart [experience], and with all your soul [tradition], and with all your mind [reason]" (Matthew 22:37). The mind and the ability to think and reason are gifts that are given by God so that human beings can observe, learn, ask questions, and come to know that they are God's children, created in God's image. God is like a loving parent who loves them unconditionally, forgives them freely, and seeks their healing and wholeness. The ability to reason gives human beings a way to live in relationship with God.

Practical theology has the power to touch lives because it opens hearts and minds to God's grace at work in the ordinariness of life. Ordinary people can understand it and, moreover, make it their own. It helps them make sense of their lives and their world. Theology that is practical is like a song that lifts the heart in praise and opens the mind to a way of living that is life-giving and life-affirming. The theology preached, taught, and lived by John and Charles Wesley touched countless lives and gave hope and purpose because it was good news.

Good News to the Poor

Theology that is genuine and faithful to the God who is revealed in Jesus, the Jew from Nazareth, always will be good news to those who are poor, struggling, oppressed, sick, and imprisoned. It is good news because it describes a God who loves unconditionally, who offers his love universally (to all), whose will for humankind is health and wholeness (shalom), and who "so loved the world that he gave his only Son, so that everyone who believes in him may not perish but may have eternal life" (John 3:16).

Theology that is faithful to the Scriptures of the Old and New Testaments describes a God who is just and righteous, who consistently identifies with and takes the side of the weak and vulnerable against the wealthy and powerful. This is good news because it reveals a God who loves and forgives all who will accept grace as the gift it is, free and without price (Isaiah 55:1). This is the theology John and Charles Wesley and the early Methodist preachers brought to the people of England and America.

This is important because our theology determines how we live and act in our daily lives. For example, the theology of the dominant culture, whose god is the market, believes that the God of Scripture is impotent and irrelevant. Therefore, everything that matters comes as a result of market forces and human effort, desire, wisdom, and greed. Science and technology have replaced God as creator and ruler of the universe, and humankind has placed itself at the focus of worship and praise. Love, forgiveness, and justice all come with a price tag. Grace is regarded as weakness. This secular theology has replaced the God of Scripture with the gods of the marketplace and technology, who demand regular sacrifice of human lives so that profits can be maximized. Those who are wealthy, healthy, and strong are the blessed ones, while those who are poor, weak, and vulnerable are the accursed.

This is an extreme example of how theology, our way of thinking about God, determines action; but it is the same reality faced by Wesley in eighteenth-century England. The dominant theology of the day was that of a distant, disinterested god who was, in the everyday concerns of life, impotent and irrelevant. In the midst of this world in which few got richer and the vast majority struggled in grinding poverty, hunger, and despair, John Wesley presented the God of Holy Scripture, the God of amazing grace. His theology was evangelical, in that it was good news to people who experienced little good in their daily lives. It was evangelical because it presented a God who is the creator of all that ever has been, all that is, and all that ever will be. This same God is the lover of their souls and bodies. Finally, Wesley's theology was evangelical because it told the story of the God who became a human being named Jesus of Nazareth, the son of a carpenter, a man who made his living with his hands. The people who heard and believed this good news were changed by it and became new people who understood themselves to be beloved children of God. As children of God, they sought to live lives that reflected God's life among them in Jesus Christ. Their theology determined the way they lived their daily lives.

This, no doubt, is why Wesley took such great care with his theological method. His goal was to bring people to faith in Christ and then to help form them as faithful disciples. His balanced method helped assure that good news was preached, taught, and lived. Beginning with Scripture and testing his ideas against the tradition of the church, personal experience and the experiences of others, and reason, Wesley's theology was good news to countless people, especially the poor. He helped them understand that they were God's children, each with a place at God's table in God's household, and that God's intention was that no one was to be excluded. Wesley understood and taught that living in God's household meant living a life that reflected the life of the head of the household. In other words, theology (belief) determined, or at least significantly influenced, the life of those who received and believed the good news offered by Wesley. These people became the people called Methodists.

A Practical Theology

As a practical theologian, Wesley never took the time to write a book that systematically laid out his theology. Instead, he wrote many sermons, tracts, and letters. He also kept a detailed journal all of his adult life. This makes perfect sense because Wesley, while certainly possessing the academic credentials of a professional theologian and churchman, could not remain confined by the academy or the church. Although he was an Oxford don (tutor and fellow), he could not be restrained by the disciplines of philosophical or scholastic theology of his day. Rather, Wesley preferred to be out with the ordinary people, particularly the poor and working classes. He visited in their homes and places of work, and he traveled the countryside on horseback, visiting towns and villages and preaching at every opportunity. Wesley's theology was a product of his experience among the people and of traveling on horseback as much as it was from the academic rigors of reading, studying, and writing. This probably is why his preaching and teaching reached the hearts of so many ordinary, poor people of his day.

One of the places we go to learn about Wesley's theology—and the place we need to go if we are to understand the theological foundation of Accountable Discipleship—is his sermons. For the remainder of this chapter, we will take a close look at one sermon in particular.

"The Scripture Way of Salvation" was written in 1765, when Wesley was sixty-two years old. He had many years and miles behind him, so this is the mature and seasoned man giving us his description of the way of salvation as it is revealed in Scripture. "The Scripture Way of Salvation" is one of Wesley's most important sermons because it provides a clear, concise means for understanding what salvation is, what faith is, and the relationship between faith and salvation. (The entire text of this sermon is printed in the Appendix, on pages 119–27.)

True to his theological method, Wesley began with Scripture. Everything he said is grounded in the Bible. The text for "The Scripture Way of Salvation" is Ephesians 2:8. In verses 1-10 we read:

> You were dead through the trespasses and sins in which you once lived, following the course of this world, following the ruler of the power of the air, the spirit that is now at work among those who are disobedient. All of us once lived among them in the passions of our flesh, following the desires of flesh and senses, and we were by nature children of wrath, like everyone else. But God, who is rich in mercy, out of the great love with which he loved us even when we were dead through our trespasses, made us alive together with Christ—by grace you have been saved—and raised us up with him and seated us with him in the heavenly places in Christ Jesus, so that in the ages to come he might show the immeasurable riches of his grace in kindness toward us in Christ Jesus. For by grace you have been saved through faith, and this is not your own doing; it is the gift of God—not the result of works, so that no one may boast. For we are what he has made us, created in Christ Jesus for good works, which God prepared beforehand to be our way of life.

We see here that the beginning and end of salvation is grace. What is grace? In a word, it is the free, unearned, unmerited gift of God's love and acceptance. This gift is given to all of humankind. It is universal and none are excluded. A simple way to describe this grace is the truth that God loves and accepts you as you are, and there is nothing you or anyone else can do about it.

This grace is made visible and tangible in Jesus Christ, who is the incarnation, the physical embodiment, of God's love for humankind. In Jesus God became human:

> Though he was in the form of God,
>   [Jesus] did not regard equality with God
>   as something to be exploited,

but emptied himself,
   taking the form of a slave,
   being born in human likeness.
And being found in human form,
   he humbled himself
   and became obedient to the
     point of death—
   even death on a cross.
               (Philippians 2:6-8)

He lived our life and died our death and rose again to defeat the powers of sin and death. By the grace given to the world in Jesus Christ, the sins of the world are forgiven and humankind is reconciled to God. In Jesus God took the initiative to restore the relationship broken by sin. This is the power of grace—the forgiveness of sin and the healing and wholeness that flows from it.

Grace is the means of salvation, which begins and ends with divine grace. It is God's work at God's initiative in Jesus Christ, crucified and risen. The means God uses to reveal this reality of grace to human beings is faith: "For by grace you have been saved through faith, and this is not your own doing; it is the gift of God" (Ephesians 2:8).

In "The Scripture Way of Salvation," Wesley wrestles with three questions that help us understand the nature of salvation, faith, and the life that flows from them:

1. What is salvation?
2. What is that faith whereby we are saved? And
3. How we are saved by it?

(From "The Scripture Way of Salvation," in *The Works of John Wesley,* Volume 2, edited by Albert C. Outler, page 156. © 1985 Abingdon Press. Used by permission.)

We will look at what Wesley has to say in response to each question. We will find in his response valuable insights into our relationship with God, with our neighbor, and with ourselves. In this sermon we find a theological framework for life in God's household that flows from Scripture, tradition, experience, and reason.

The Scripture Way of Salvation

Wesley begins the sermon by acknowledging that theologians and church fathers and mothers have made religion much more complicated and difficult to understand than it really is. Perhaps he is confirming that some centuries of tradition and speculation have rendered Christian faith incomprehensible to ordinary people. This is important because Wesley's audience was the ordinary man and woman on the street. They were not highly educated, and many were illiterate. Their understanding of the world was concrete and simple. Wesley comes to them with the good news that the essence of Christian religion is really quite simple.

> Yet how easy to be understood, how plain and simple a thing, is the genuine religion of Jesus Christ! Provided only that we take it in its native form, just as it is described in the oracles of God. It is exactly suited by the wise Creator and Governor of the world to the weak understanding and narrow capacity of man in his present state. How observable is this both with regard to the end it proposes and the means to attain that end! The end is, in one word, salvation: the means to attain it, faith.
>
> (From "The Scripture Way of Salvation," in *The Works of John Wesley,* Volume 2, edited by Albert C. Outler, pages 155–56. © 1985 Abingdon Press. Used by permission.)

This is reassuring to us today as well. We live in a culture in which many people in the church have had little or no experience with Christian tradition. People come to the church because they are spiritually hungry and are therefore searching for meaning and purpose in their lives. They sense an emptiness they know cannot be filled by what the world has to offer. Wesley assures us that God's good news for the world in Jesus Christ is available and accessible to everyone.

What Is Salvation?

In the Scriptures, the Greek word that often is translated as "saved" is also translated as "to be healed" or "to be made whole." This important word, *sozo,* helps us understand the Christian meaning of salvation. To be saved is to be set free from sin (separation and alienation from God), to be restored to a right relationship with God, and to have the brokenness of your heart and life restored to wholeness. All this has been done for you by God in Jesus Christ.

Wesley begins the sermon by telling us what salvation is not:

> The salvation which is here spoken of is not what is frequently understood by that word, the going to heaven, eternal happiness. It is not the soul's going to paradise... It is not a blessing which lies on the other side death, or (as we usually speak) in the other world.
>
> (From "The Scripture Way of Salvation," in *The Works of John Wesley,* Volume 2, edited by Albert C. Outler, page 156. © 1985 Abingdon Press. Used by permission.)

Wesley dispels the notion that salvation is something that we can look forward to only after death. He removes the limitations popular culture has placed on it. Salvation is a future promise and hope; however, the Scriptures are clear that it also is a present reality. Salvation is both here now and a future promise.

Wesley's justification for his claim is Ephesians 2:8, where the writer tells us: "Ye are saved." (The New Revised Standard Version renders this verse: "You have been saved.") Wesley wants us to notice that the writer does not say: "You will be saved" or "You may be saved." Salvation is a gift given for the present that draws those who receive it into the future. It is important to Wesley and Paul that we understand salvation as being both a present reality and a future promise, because if we regard it as solely in the future, it is too easy to believe that we have earned or gained it by our own effort. Wesley and Paul clearly state that salvation is a gift from God and is entirely God's doing. If that is so, then it must be both a present reality and a future promise. It is more about our being than it is about our doing.

After establishing salvation as a present fact, Wesley immediately grounds it in grace. Not only is salvation a gift, but, because it is grounded in grace, it also is available to all people. God initiates the process of salvation by giving human beings the ability to act like children of God.

> If we take this in its utmost extent it will include all that is wrought in the soul by what is frequently termed "natural conscience," but more properly, "preventing grace"; all the "drawings" of "the Father," the desires after God, which, if we yield to them, increase more and more; all that "light" wherewith the Son of God "enlighteneth everyone that cometh into the world," *showing* every [person] "to do justly, to love mercy, and to walk humbly with [his or her] God"; all the *convictions* which [the] Spirit from time to time works in every child of man.
>
> (From "The Scripture Way of Salvation," in *The Works of John Wesley,* Volume 2, edited by Albert C. Outler, pages 156–57. © 1985 Abingdon Press. Used by permission.)

Preventing (also called prevenient) grace is the presence and power of God that is with us before we are aware of God's existence. It is the grace that goes before, preparing our hearts to receive God's gift of Jesus Christ. In this sense, we may call it preparing grace.

Preparing grace awakens the heart and mind to God's presence and power in the world around us and in our lives. As we are awakened, our human condition becomes more acute, and grace opens our eyes to our own sinfulness. It also helps us know that the only cure for our brokenness is God, as God is revealed in the crucified and risen Jesus Christ. In other words, preparing grace is God's hand bringing us to faith. In household terms, it brings us to the porch and gets us ready to receive the forgiveness and acceptance of God through Jesus Christ (the door) and to enter God's household of faith.

Conversely, preparing grace also gives us the freedom to say no to God, which is the other side of God's grace. Because God respects our humanity and integrity, God gives us, by grace, the freedom and power to say no to the gift of salvation. In this sense, God's grace is not irresistible. Likewise, this freedom also is an expression of God's amazing love, in that God does not force anyone to accept the gift of salvation. And this in no way limits God's love only to those who say yes. God continues to love those who say no. And preparing grace continues to act with, in, and around them until the last day, when the gates to the kingdom of God are closed. On that day, at the end of history, if there is even one place empty at the heavenly banquet, if even one person has persisted in saying no and excluded him or herself from the heavenly feast, the feast will begin in silence because the Host will be weeping.

After Wesley deals with the preliminaries, he describes salvation:

> But we are at present concerned only with that salvation which the Apostle [Paul] is directly speaking of. And this consists of two general parts, justification and sanctification.
>
> Justification is another word for pardon. It is the forgiveness of all our sins, and (what is necessarily implied therein) our acceptance with God. The price whereby this hath been procured for us...is the blood and righteousness of Christ, or (to express it a little more clearly) all that Christ hath done and suffered for us till "he poured out his soul for the transgressors."
>
> (From "The Scripture Way of Salvation," in *The Works of John Wesley,* Volume 2, edited by Albert C. Outler, pages 157–58. © 1985 Abingdon Press. Used by permission.)

Salvation consists of two equally important parts: justification and sanctification. These are biblical words that describe the process God sets in motion within the human being through the grace and power of the Holy Spirit. They are God's work for and with each person whose eyes and heart are opened to God by prevenient (preparing) grace. In other words, prevenient grace is God's work of preparing the human heart and life for justification and sanctification.

Justification and Justifying Grace

What is justification? A discussion of justification must begin with an understanding of sin because justification is God's work of overcoming the effects of human sin. The Scriptures tell us that sin is separation and alienation from God (Psalm 1; Romans 1:18-23). Some of the consequences of sin are disobedience to the law of God, guilt, and a life that is destructive to the self and the world. Sin is part of human nature. It is a self-centered and selfish way of living. It deceives the heart and mind into believing the self is all that matters in life, that the self is the center of the universe, and that fulfillment in life comes from serving the self to the exclusion of all others, especially God. Sin dwells deep in every human heart and is the aspect of human nature that leads to all that is evil in the world. Sin distorts and disfigures the image of God that dwells in every human heart. It is like a cancer that eats away at the heart and life of each human being and community. Sin destroys life and community. The only cure for this disease is God and God's love given to the world in Jesus Christ.

Wesley tells us justification is God's pardon, God's forgiveness of all our sins. Justification is the restoration of our relationship with God. The obstacles placed between us and God (sins) have been removed and the way made for us to take a step toward God. We can see an illustration of this when we look at a sunflower. When the sun rises in the morning or clouds break up on an overcast day, allowing the bright sunshine to reach the earth, sunflowers immediately begin to turn their faces toward the sun. As the sun travels across the sky, the flowers follow it. They are justified; they are in alignment with the sun and go where the sun leads them. In much the same way, we follow the Son of God when we are justified by his grace.

Justification brings about a relative change in the human heart and life. It changes our alignment away from sin and death and toward God and the life-giving waters of his grace. When a person is justified, he or she is set free from the powers of sin and death. The person's life is brought into alignment with the life of Jesus Christ. Justifying grace equips us with what we need to begin to learn how to walk with Christ.

Justification is a gift from God. As Wesley says,

> The price whereby this [justification] hath been procured for us…is the blood and righteousness of Christ, or (to express it a little more clearly) all that Christ hath done and suffered for us till "he poured out his soul for the transgressors."
>
> (From "The Scripture Way of Salvation," in *The Works of John Wesley*, Volume 2, edited by Albert C. Outler, pages 157–58. © 1985 Abingdon Press. Used by permission.)

In other words, the life (righteousness), death, and resurrection (blood) of Christ are the source of our restored relationship with God. Christ's righteousness has made us righteous in God's eyes. He took all the sins of the world on himself on the cross. He took your sins and mine and all the sins of humankind (past, present, and future) into the wounds of his hands, feet, and side. The powers of sin and death were swallowed up in the love of God in Christ Jesus, crucified and risen.

"Death has been swallowed up in victory."
"Where, O death, is your victory?
 Where, O death, is your sting?"

The sting of death is sin, and the power of sin is the law. But thanks be to God, who gives us the victory through our Lord Jesus Christ.

Therefore, my beloved, be steadfast, immovable, always excelling in the work of the Lord, because you know that in the Lord your labor is not in vain.   (1 Corinthians 15:54b-58)

But he was wounded for our
    transgressions,
  crushed for our iniquities;
upon him was the punishment that
    made us whole,
  and by his bruises we are healed.
              (Isaiah 53:5)

This is grace, amazing grace! In Christ's life, death, and resurrection, God has removed the blockage of sin and given us the way to a restored relationship with God. Justifying grace gives human beings the power to accept this love and participate in this relationship. This is the first step on the way of salvation.

Sanctification and Sanctifying Grace

What is sanctification? It is another of those biblical/theological words that so often are used and misunderstood. Quite simply, sanctification is the process whereby God makes us holy. To be sanctified is to be made holy. For Wesley, to be made holy is to "be perfect...as your heavenly Father is perfect" (Matthew 5:48). By this he means that by grace we can be made perfect in love (Colossians 3:14; 1 John 4:19). To be holy is to love as God loves. It does not mean that we never make a mistake or never sin, but that all that we do and say is done in love. To be holy is to be motivated only by God and God's love for the world in Jesus Christ. Another way of describing holiness and Christian perfection is maturity of faith and life. To be holy is to be grown up in the faith and grace of Christ. This, for Wesley, is the goal of Christian faith. Wesley puts it this way:

And at the same time that we are justified, yea, in that very moment, *sanctification* begins. In that instant we are "born again," "born from above," "born of the Spirit." There is a *real* as well as a *relative* change. We are inwardly renewed by the power of God. We feel the "love of God shed abroad in our heart by the Holy Ghost which is given unto us," producing love to all [humankind], and more especially to the children of

God; expelling the love of the world, the love of pleasure, of ease, of honour, of money; together with pride, anger, self-will, and every other evil temper—in a word, changing the "earthly, sensual, devilish" mind into "the mind which was in Christ Jesus."

(From "The Scripture Way of Salvation," in *The Works of John Wesley*, Volume 2, edited by Albert C. Outler, page 158. © 1985 Abingdon Press. Used by permission.)

As justification brings about a relative change (a new alignment with God), sanctification causes a real, inward change. Justification changes the person's relationship to and with God. Sanctification changes the person. The apostle Paul describes the change in 2 Corinthians 5:17: "So if anyone is in Christ, there is a new creation: everything old has passed away; see, everything has become new!"

A way to understand what happens in sanctification is imagining a caterpillar in its cocoon. Over time a process of transformation takes place. When the time is right, the cocoon opens and a butterfly emerges. A real change has occurred; the caterpillar has become a butterfly. It also is helpful to know that the butterfly is the mature form of the creature that begins life as a caterpillar. In much the same way, sanctification is the maturation process God works in human beings to transform them into mature daughters and sons.

This is what Jesus was talking about when he told Nicodemus, "Very truly, I tell you, no one can see the kingdom of God without being born from above" (John 3:3). The new birth is the beginning of sanctification. It is God working in the justified heart to bring a new life out of the old. The old self is set aside, and a new self is born. A real change occurs in the person's character.

In household terms, justification is the door, and sanctification is the house. Prevenient grace brings a person to the porch of the household of faith. Justifying grace helps a person open the door to the house. Sanctifying grace enables the person to step across the threshold and into the house itself. It makes the way for him or her to begin exploring the household of faith that has been opened by God's amazing grace.

Sanctification is the process of restoring and healing the image of God that is part of each human being. The restored divine image is unrestrained love of God and neighbor. In the process, one grows in the likeness of Christ. This is the work and action of God, but it requires our cooperation. God empowers and enables us in the process of obedience to the law of God. (This is summarized by Jesus in Matthew 22:37-40: "'You shall love the Lord your God with all your heart, and with all your soul, and with all your mind.... You shall love your neighbor as yourself.' On these two commandments hang all the law and the prophets.") Sanctification is the way that moves us closer and closer to God and, in the process, forms us into the image of Christ. It is the means by which God empowers us to become the people God created us to be.

> From the time of our being "born again" the gradual work of sanctification takes place. We are enabled "by the Spirit" to "mortify the deeds of the body," of our evil nature. And as we are more and more dead to sin, we are more and more alive to God. We go on from grace to grace, while we are careful to "abstain from all appearance of evil," and are "zealous of good works," "as we have opportunity doing good to all [people]"; while we walk in all his ordinances blameless, therein worshipping him in spirit and in truth; while we take up our cross and deny ourselves every pleasure that does not lead us to God.
>
> (From "The Scripture Way of Salvation," in *The Works of John Wesley,* Volume 2, edited by Albert C. Outler, page 160. © 1985 Abingdon Press. Used by permission.)

The Faith Through Which We Are Saved

Wesley believed we are saved by grace through faith. The way of salvation is God working in and with each human being. Wesley believed that grace is co-operant, which means that God loves human beings in a way that respects our dignity and personhood. God does not force salvation on anyone. It is God's gift freely given that must be accepted. God wants us to cooperate with his grace and to participate in the life of Christ.

Faith is the beginning of our cooperation with God. It is our response to God's initiative for and with us. Faith is a twofold response to God. First, faith is a gift from God.

> [Faith is] a kind of spiritual *light* exhibited to the soul, and a supernatural *sight* or perception thereof. Accordingly the Scripture speaks sometimes of God's giving light, sometimes a power of discerning it. So St. Paul: "God, who commanded light to shine out of darkness, hath shined in our hearts, to give us the light of the knowledge of the glory of God in the face of Jesus Christ." And elsewhere the same Apostle speaks "of the eyes of" our "understanding being opened." By this twofold operation of the Holy Spirit—having the eyes of our soul both *opened* and *enlightened*—we see the things which the natural "eye hath not seen, neither the ear heard."
>
> (From "The Scripture Way of Salvation," in *The Works of John Wesley,* Volume 2, edited by Albert C. Outler, pages 160–61. © 1985 Abingdon Press. Used by permission.)

Here, faith is described as being like a light shining in the darkness of the world's sin and brokenness. The darkness blinds human beings to the reality of God's light and love. Humans walk around doing their best to make their way through the darkness. In actuality, the darkness is our own because our eyes are closed. One day when, by prevenient (preparing) and justifying (accepting) grace, we hear and accept the good news of God in Jesus Christ, we suddenly discover that when we open our eyes, we can see the world as it really is, bathed in the light of God that is Christ (John 1:5). Faith comes through the experience of his good news and by grace, opening our eyes to see the presence and power of God at work in our lives and in the world:

> Faith is a divine evidence and conviction, not only that "God was in Christ, reconciling the world unto himself," but also that Christ "loved *me,* and gave himself for *me."* It is by this faith (whether we term it the *essence,* or rather a *property* thereof) that we "receive Christ."
>
> (From "The Scripture Way of Salvation," in *The Works of John Wesley,* Volume 2, edited by Albert C. Outler, page 161. © 1985 Abingdon Press. Used by permission.)

Second, and following this assurance that we are a child of God, faith is also a confidence and trust in God. It is our assent and belief in God's goodness, power, and love. The writer of Hebrews says:

> Now faith is the assurance of things hoped for, the conviction of things not seen.... By faith we understand that the worlds were prepared by the word of God, so that what is seen was made from things that are not visible.
>
> (Hebrews 11:1, 3)

This faith flows from the experience of God as the loving parent who gives us the confidence and trust we need to open our eyes and see the world as it really is, free from the blinders of sin and death. Through faith we are saved—justified and sanctified.

It is important for us to understand that faith in and of itself is a work of God's grace in and with us. It is not something we do by our own power or will. Faith is a gift from God through which we are able to experience, believe, and trust in God and God's goodness, justice, and righteousness. It is the kind of gift that must be used. Like a candle or a light bulb, faith must be used for it to be effective. It illuminates our world so that we can see it as God meant it to be seen. Faith comes to us by grace as a precious gift to open our heart and guide our life in the way of Christ in the world. It is the means of our salvation.

How Are We Justified and Sanctified?

We now come to the third and final section of "The Scripture Way of Salvation." It is here that Wesley puts his understanding of the way of salvation together. He has established the foundation (Scripture revealed and held together by grace) and laid out the pieces (justification, sanctification, and faith). The sermon has helped us understand that we are saved by grace through faith. Grace is universal: It is for all of God's creatures. Grace is prevenient: It is at work within and around us before we are aware of it, preparing our heart and awakening our spirit to our own brokenness and emptiness. It brings us to an awareness of how lost we really are and that God, who comes to us in Jesus Christ, is the one who will lead us home. Grace is justifying: It restores the relationship with God that has been broken by sin. Grace is sanctifying: It empowers us to live the life we were created to live, the life of Christ. This grace restores within us the image of God and works with us as God forms our character into oneness with the character of Christ. In other words, by grace we will become holy. This is entirely God's work for and with us. Salvation is God's work, but because God respects our integrity as individuals, God does not impose or force salvation on anyone. Therefore, we need to cooperate with God as we are being saved by grace.

Faith is the essential means of our cooperation with God's saving work on our behalf. Wesley says,

> Faith is the condition, and the only condition, of justification. It is the condition: none is justified but he that believes; without faith no man is justified. And it is the only condition: this alone is sufficient for justification. Everyone that believes is justified, whatever else he has or has not. In other words: no man is justified till he believes; every man when he believes is justified.
>
> (From "The Scripture Way of Salvation," in *The Works of John Wesley,* Volume 2, edited by Albert C. Outler, page 162. © 1985 Abingdon Press. Used by permission.)

He repeats himself so many times here to make sure that his readers understand that faith is the only condition of our justification, that we cannot be justified by anything we do on our own. No amount of good works or being good will make God accept us. God's acceptance and love are a gift, and our relationship with God has been made secure through the life, death, and resurrection of Jesus Christ. It is entirely God's doing on behalf of the world (John 3:16-17).

Wesley wants to make this clear, in order to dispel the notion that anyone can win God's favor by his or her own goodness or strength of character. The work of justification has already been done for every single human being ever born and everyone who ever will be born. And the only condition on receiving and participating in the life God offers with Christ is faith, nothing more and nothing less.

Wesley asks the question that you may be asking yourself:

But does not God command us to *repent* also? Yea, and to "bring forth fruits meet for repentance"? To "cease," for instance, "from doing evil," and "learn to do well"? And is not both the one and the other of the utmost necessity? Insomuch that if we willingly neglect either we cannot reasonably expect to be justified at all? But if this be so, how can it be said that faith is the only condition of justification?

(From "The Scripture Way of Salvation," in *The Works of John Wesley*, Volume 2, edited by Albert C. Outler, page 162. © 1985 Abingdon Press. Used by permission.)

His response is a resounding yes. God does require us to repent and "bring forth fruits meet [befitting] for repentance"; however, repentance is not a condition of our justification. Our relationship to God is not dependent on repentance. Wesley is saying that repentance is our appropriate response to the grace we receive through justification and faith in Jesus Christ. When we are justified, God enables us to turn away from our life of sin (self-centered, materialistic, and greedy) and turn toward Christ (self-giving, life-affirming, and thankful). This is repentance, which simply means to turn around. When we repent we make a 180-degree turn away from the world and toward the God revealed to us in Jesus Christ. In so doing, we orient our life in such a way that we strive to obey his commands to love God with all that we are and all that we have, and to love our neighbor as ourselves. This is true repentance.

The repentance that flows from faith and a living relationship with Jesus Christ compels us to do good. It empowers us to want to follow the commands of Christ: "Love the Lord your God with all your heart, and with all your soul, and with all your mind" (Matthew 22:37); "Love your neighbor as yourself" (Matthew 22:39); and "Just as I have loved you, you also should love one another. By this everyone will know that you are my disciples, if you have love for one another" (John 13:34b-35). When we repent, we turn away from serving the world and our selfish interests and turn toward serving Christ and his interests. To serve Christ in the world is "to do justice, and to love kindness, and to walk humbly with [our] God" (Micah 6:8). When we are justified, God lets us know that our sins are forgiven, we are loved unconditionally, and we are set free for repentance and to serve Christ in the world.

Our justification is not conditioned on our repentance or our good works. The only condition is faith. Repentance and good works are necessary for those who have time and opportunity. In other words, people who accept God's love and the gift of faith on their deathbed will be justified and sanctified. They have neither time nor opportunity for repentance and the works representative of repentance. This is not to say that obedience and continued repentance are optional for those who choose to live as justified and sanctified disciples. Just as faith is the only condition for obtaining justification, works of obedience to the commands of Christ and continued repentance are the conditions for keeping it.

What about sanctification? After dealing with justification by faith, Wesley poses the question he often was asked: "But do you believe we are sanctified by faith?" Wesley responds:

> Exactly as we are justified by faith, so are we sanctified by faith. Faith is the condition, and the only condition of sanctification, exactly as it is of justification. It is the condition: none is sanctified but he that believes; without faith no man is sanctified. And it is the only condition: this alone is sufficient for sanctification. Everyone that believes is sanctified, whatever else he has or has not. In other words: no man is sanctified till he believes; every man when he believes is sanctified.
>
> (From "The Scripture Way of Salvation," in *The Works of John Wesley,* Volume 2, edited by Albert C. Outler, pages 163–64. © 1985 Abingdon Press. Used by permission.)

At the moment we are justified, we also are sanctified. Put more precisely, the process of sanctification begins with justification. And faith is the only condition that enables us to participate in God's work for, with, and within us by grace.

When a person is justified and sanctified, this does not mean that he or she is free from sin. That person's sins are forgiven, but he or she is not entirely free of sin's power and temptation. Sin remains lurking at the door waiting for an opportunity to once again take up residence in the person's heart.

This is why the repentance subsequent to justification is so essential. Grace continues to work with the person after justification, in order to help him or her remain on the path with Christ, to learn how to live in God's house and obey the household rules. The reality of all human life, even for those who have responded to God's initiative and are justified and sanctified, is that they must live in a world that is ruled by sin (expressed as violence, greed, jealousy, hatred). This makes repentance all the more important.

> One thing more is implied in this repentance, namely, a conviction of our helplessness, of our utter inability to think one good thought, or to form one good desire; and much more to speak one word aright, or to perform one good action but through his free, almighty grace, first preventing us, and then accompanying us every moment.
>
> (From "The Scripture Way of Salvation," in *The Works of John Wesley,* Volume 2, edited by Albert C. Outler, page 166. © 1985 Abingdon Press. Used by permission.)

Christ walks with us. In the process of sanctification, we must look to Christ daily for guidance and forgiveness. He is the one who leads and empowers us to resist temptation and to do good. He gives us the grace we need to obey his commandments and to grow into his likeness more and more each day, in spite of the sin that continues to dwell within our heart.

Wesley teaches that sanctification is both instantaneous and a process in which we participate over time with God. It is instantaneous in that it begins at the moment of justification. Our sins are forgiven and God adopts us as God's own beloved children. We are "born again" or "born from above." This means that at the moment of justification we are sanctified and become like a newborn infant. And like all newborns, we require care and nurture in order to grow. We cannot remain an infant; we must either grow in faith and grace or die. By faith God empowers us to cooperate with and participate in Christ's life in the world. He makes clear that we are justified and sanctified by faith, but that we must engage in good works if we are to keep our salvation.

> It is incumbent on all that are justified to be zealous of good works. And these are so necessary that if a man willingly neglect them, he cannot reasonably expect that he shall ever be sanctified. He cannot "grow in grace," in the image of God, the mind which was in Christ Jesus; nay, he cannot retain the grace he has received, he cannot continue in faith, or in the favour of God.
>
> What is the inference we must draw herefrom? Why, that both repentance, rightly understood, and the practice of all good works, works of piety, as well as works of mercy (now properly so called, since they spring from faith) are in some sense necessary to sanctification.
>
> (From "The Scripture Way of Salvation," in *The Works of John Wesley,* Volume 2, edited by Albert C. Outler, page 164. © 1985 Abingdon Press. Used by permission.)

There is a delicate balance here. We must be clear that these required good works are in no way related to our being justified and sanctified. They are, however, subsequent to justification and sanctification. Wesley is adamant in affirming that we are justified and sanctified by grace through faith, and faith alone. Faith is the only condition. The doing of good works is necessary for faith to continue and grow. Without them, faith dies along with our life with God.

If you accept the gift of God's amazing grace (justification), if you desire to be a child of God and to live in God's household (sanctification), then you need to live by the rules of that household. The rules, as we have stated above, are quite simple and straightforward: love God and love your neighbor as yourself. These are what Wesley and the early Methodists meant when they referred to the need for works of piety and works of mercy. The need for the good works are taken directly from the life of Jesus and the early church. They are how we are to "let the same mind be in [us] that was in Christ Jesus" and to "work out [our] own salvation with fear and trembling; for it is God who is at work in [us], enabling [us] both to will and to work for his good pleasure" (Philippians 2:5, 12). The faith God gives empowers God's children to live lives conformed to the life of Jesus Christ. Faith enables us to obey Jesus' commands to love God, to love our neighbor as ourselves, and to love one another as he has loved us (Matthew 22:37-40; John 13:34-35).

How do we live out our love of God? We incorporate the means of grace into our daily lives. Works of piety (acts of worship and devotion) are the instituted means of grace, the things we do with God in private (acts of devotion) and in public (acts of worship). Prayer (personal and with family or friends), reading and studying the Bible, attending worship services, receiving the Lord's Supper, participating in a small group for mutual support and accountability, and fasting or abstinence are instituted means of grace because they were normative parts of Jesus' life and the life of the early church.

Works of mercy are the prudential means of grace, the acts of compassion and justice that are loving your neighbor as yourself. We do them because they are a reflection of the life and character of God in Jesus Christ. They are the ways in which we love our neighbor as ourselves. What are the prudential, or practical, means of grace? Jesus describes them in Matthew 25:35-40:

> "For I was hungry and you gave me food, I was thirsty and you gave me something to drink, I was a stranger and you welcomed me, I was naked and you gave me clothing, I was sick and you took care of me, I was in prison and you visited me." Then the righteous will answer him, "Lord, when was it that we saw you hungry and gave you food, or thirsty and gave you something to drink? And when was it that we saw you a stranger and welcomed you, or naked and gave you clothing? And when was it that we saw you sick or in prison and visited you?" And the king will answer them, "Truly I tell you, just as you did it to one of the least of these who are members of my family, you did it to me."

These practical means of grace are as important and essential for maintaining our relationship with God (sanctification) as are the instituted means of grace. Wesley regarded "doing good" as essential to a Christian's spiritual well-being. Jesus is clear in Matthew 25 that when we engage in acts of compassion and justice, we are serving him.

He is with the poor, the refugees, the prisoners, the sick, the residents of nursing homes, the weak, and the vulnerable. This is why Wesley spent all of his adult life in ministry with and for the poor and voiceless people of eighteenth-century England. He was a vocal opponent of slavery, war, and the exploitation of the poor. He was an advocate of providing adequate healthcare, affordable housing, and education for the poor and their children. Not only was he an advocate, but he also personally participated in the lives of the poor by visiting in their homes, eating meals with them, and becoming their friend. Christ's teaching and life is clear that when we become friends of the poor, we become friends of Christ.

These instituted and prudential means of grace are found in Scripture because they are necessary for maintaining our relationship with God. When we cease to do them, our relationship with God suffers. They are called means of grace because they connect us with God and God's grace. In other words, the means of grace help make us available to God. The more available to God we become, the more God is able to form us into the image of Christ.

An illustration to help us understand the nature and means of grace is that of the wind and a sailboat at sea. Grace is like the wind, which is powerful and blows on everyone equally. It cannot be seen, but it can be felt and put to use. The crew members of a sailboat work together to raise the sails and orient them in just the right way to catch the wind, which propels the boat forward to its destination. For this to work, the sailors depend on one another working as a team to keep the sails full and the boat on course. We are like the sailors on the boat. Some are seasoned and experienced in the ways of the wind (grace). They can tell when the wind is changing by watching the water and trusting their senses. They work with the wind to reach their destination. The experienced ones also have the responsibility of teaching those who perhaps have never sailed before or those who have some experience but have much more to learn. The crew learns to trust, support, and depend on one another as they grow in understanding of the wind and its power to take them where they want to go. Grace working in human lives is co-operant. Like a sailboat crew that learns to cooperate with the wind to bring them to their destination, human beings learn to cooperate with God and God's grace as they are being saved. Another way of understanding the connection between salvation and daily life (discipleship) is that of a household. Each member of the family is loved and accepted, and everyone has a responsibility to the family and the head of the household. Everyone has a job to do.

The means of grace (works of piety and works of mercy) are the tools God has given to humankind to help us learn about God and to make ourselves available to receiving and sharing God's grace. Grace that is not shared is impotent. Grace, by its nature, needs to flow freely like the wind from one person to another. In this way we participate in our own salvation and in the salvation of the world.

Conclusion

John Wesley's theology; his understanding of God, Jesus Christ, the Holy Spirit; the tradition of the church; and his life experience determined the way Wesley lived his life. His theology compelled him to travel the countryside and cities of England, preaching the good news of God in Jesus Christ, crucified and risen. Wesley's study of the Scriptures and the teachings of the fathers and mothers of the church led him to believe that the God of the universe is characterized by grace. The grace of God is universal; it is for all people and all of creation. It works in the lives of people before they are aware of God and God's love for them, preparing them for a life-changing encounter with Jesus Christ. Grace draws people to faith and salvation through Jesus Christ. It brings them to a restored relationship with God, in which they know that their sins are forgiven and that God's will for them is wholeness and peace. Grace empowers people to live the life they were created to live. It enables them to turn away from the powers of the world that lead to death and forms them, over time, into the image of Christ. It helps them grow from infants in the faith to mature grownups. Wesley has much to teach us today about living as disciples of Jesus Christ and as children in God's household.

The General Rule of Discipleship and Covenant Discipleship Groups are important tools that help you and your church experience and grow in God's amazing, saving grace.

For Reflection and Discussion

1. You are a theologian if you think and talk about God, your relationship with God, and God's relationship with humankind. Why, do you think, has theology become suspect in many churches today? What is preventing people of faith from doing theology? How does your theology affect the way you live your life?
2. What are the four pillars of Wesley's practical theology? What makes this balanced approach to doing theology practical?
3. Why is genuine Christian theology good news to the poor?

4. Read Ephesians 2:1-10 aloud to yourself or to your group. What does the passage say about God? What does the passage say about human beings? What does the passage say about the relationship between God and human beings? What does the passage say about you and your relationship with God?
5. How would you define sin?
6. How does salvation, or being saved by grace through faith, influence your daily life?
7. How would you define grace? How have you experienced grace?
8. Describe your experience of prevenient grace. Why is it so important?
9. What is faith? What difference does it make in your life and relationships?
10. What do justification and sanctification mean to you? How are they related? What do justification and sanctification have to do with your daily life? your place in the church? your relationship with your family, friends, neighbors, and the world?
11. What are the means of grace? What is the difference between instituted means of grace and prudential means of grace? Why are they essential to the life of a disciple?
12. What is the meaning of the term *responsible grace*? Does responsibility come with the gift of grace? Describe your responsibility.

To Learn More

"Christian Perfection," by John Wesley, in *The Works of John Wesley,* Volume 2, edited by Albert C. Outler (Nashville: Abingdon Press, 1985), pages 97–124.

Grace & Responsibility: A Wesleyan Theology for Today, by John B. Cobb, Jr. (Nashville: Abingdon Press, 1995).

John Wesley, edited by Albert C. Outler (New York: Oxford University Press, reprint edition 1981).

John Wesley's Sermons: An Anthology, edited by Albert C. Outler and Richard P. Heitzenrater (Nashville: Abingdon Press, 1991).

Methodist Doctrine: The Essentials, by Ted A. Campbell (Nashville: Abingdon Press, 1999).

Practical Divinity: Readings in Wesleyan Theology (Volumes 1 and 2), edited by Thomas A. Langford (Nashville: Abingdon Press, 1999).

Responsible Grace: John Wesley's Practical Theology, by Randy L. Maddox (Nashville: Kingswood Books, 1994).

The New Creation: John Wesley's Theology Today, by Theodore Runyon (Nashville: Abingdon Press, 1998).

The Scripture Way of Salvation: The Heart of John Wesley's Theology, by Kenneth J. Collins (Nashville: Abingdon Press, 1997).

Wesley and Sanctification: A Study in the Doctrine of Salvation, by Harald Lindström (Nappanee, IN: Evangel Publishing House, second edition 1996).

Chapter 4

The Family Story: John Wesley and the People Called Methodists

The Bible is the story of God's household. In the Bible we read of what God has done in the past and what God promises to do now and in the future. The Bible tells us the history of God's relationship with the world through the people of Israel and through Jesus Christ. In its pages we discover who we are and whose we are.

Theology is how human beings think and talk and write about God. It is the story of how we come into God's household and live as members of God's family. It is how we find our story in God's story.

Like all families, the household of God has many different and diverse branches. The members are related to one another. Each member is grounded in and part of God's story, with his or her own unique story within the big Story. The members of the various family branches share an understanding of their relationship with the Head of the Household that distinguishes them from the others. No story is more or less authentic than the others, and each helps people understand the relationship they share with God (the Head of the Household), with the other members of the branch, and with the greater family.

These family branches are what we today call denominations. They are the many diverse expressions of faithful relationship with the God who was revealed to the world in the Jew from Nazareth, Jesus Christ.

Each came about because of varying interpretations of Scripture, tradition, religious experience, and/or understanding of God and God's relationship with the world.

The diversity of Christian religious expression is a reflection of the diversity of the human experience of God, God's creation and life in it. It reveals the truth that God is a God who acts in and through human history. History teaches that each human being has a part and place in God's story. History is important because we need to know where we have been before we can get a clear understanding of where God is leading us. Just like a family whose history tells each member, and the world, who they are and who they are not, the history of the people called Methodists tells those of us who claim them as our ancestors who we are and who we are not. The history of the Methodists is a rich and inspiring story filled with drama, power, and disappointment. As we look at this history, we will learn who the people called Methodists were and, I hope, will gain a vision of who the United Methodists can become.

There is much in the past that can help us move forward into God's future. Knowing who our ancestors were helps us gain a better, deeper understanding of who we are today and who we can become in the future. For most of my life I had little knowledge of who my ancestors were. Members of my family on my father's side never spoke much about who the Manskars were or where they came from. I knew that my mother's side of the family (Tallaksons) came from Norway around the turn of the twentieth century. No one seemed to know where the Manskars came from. That is, until we discovered a distant relative who had a passion for genealogy. He had spent years doing research and compiling information on the family name. I learned from the data he had gathered that the Manskars originated in a small town in Germany and came to America in the mid-eighteenth century. Some of them fought in the Revolutionary War. Later, they were some of the earliest settlers of Tennessee, the place I now call home. When I gained that little bit of knowledge of my family story, I gained a better understanding of who I am and my place in my family's story.

I had a similar experience in seminary when I studied John Wesley and the early Methodists. For the first time in my life I learned the story of the faith tradition within which I had grown up. In the process I discovered who the people called Methodists were. They were men and women whose lives were centered in Christ and who sought to allow Christ to form their hearts and their lives to be like his. As I learned more about those Methodists and the Wesleys, my understanding of who God was calling me to become as a disciple of Jesus Christ became clearer.

In this chapter we will take a brief look at the history of the early years of the branch of God's family called Methodists. We will get to know the men through whom God worked to lead, organize, and inspire the Methodists: Rev. John Wesley and his brother Rev. Charles Wesley. We will see how the Wesleys applied their experience with God and God's way of salvation to help others come to know God and enter into life in God's household through small groups known as class meetings. Learning the history of the Methodists will help the United Methodists of today gain a clearer understanding of who we are and our place in the story of life in God's household.

John Wesley's World

The place to begin is a description of the world in which the Wesleys and the early Methodists lived: England in the eighteenth century. This is important to us today because, as we will see, there were many similarities between then and now. The eighteenth century was a time of dramatic social, economic, and technological change. It was an age of discovery and transition. While there are significant differences, there are equally significant similarities to our world, which is why we can look to the early Methodists to learn about a way of discipleship for today.

The culture and economy were changing from agrarian to industrial, for the eighteenth century was an age of scientific and technological progress that enabled the development of large-scale industries: coal mining, fabric milling, armament and machine manufacturing, and so forth. The growth of factories attracted to the cities people from the rural regions and towns who were searching for jobs and higher wages. What they found were factory and mill jobs that demanded long hours of hard, dirty, grinding labor. As a result, the population of the towns and cities began to grow; but they had little or no services (housing, healthcare, water, sewerage) to meet the growing needs of the new population. Consequently, the many workers and their families lived in conditions that can be described only as squalor.

The gulf between rich and poor, which was great, became deeper and wider. While the rise of industry and mercantilism gave more people access to wealth, it also left many behind. The rich got richer. The middle class became an economic and cultural presence for the first time in history. And the poor got poorer. The poor provided the labor that produced the increasing wealth of the rich. The lack of education and access to resources and the cultural and religious attitudes toward poverty kept them poor.

The eighteenth century was a time of striking scientific, philosophical, and social discovery. It was the beginning of the intellectual, philosophical, and scientific movement known as the Enlightenment that has formed the understanding of the world we know today. At the foundation of Enlightenment thinking is empiricism, which, stated simply, says that before any idea or belief can be accepted, it must provide observable evidence for its claims. Because there is no empirical evidence for the existence (or nonexistence) of God, many people educated by Enlightenment principles came to believe that faith was a futile pursuit. The rise of science and philosophy moved God from the center to the margins of eighteenth-century culture.

The Church of England was the official, established church. While there were a number of other denominations known as dissenters (Presbyterians, Congregationalists, Baptists, and Quakers), the vast majority of the citizens of England were members of the established church. The Church of England traces its origins to King Henry VIII (1491–1547), who separated from the Catholic Church when the Pope refused to grant him a divorce. The Church of England, also known as the Anglican Church, was neither Roman Catholic nor Protestant. Its liturgy and theology were known as "the middle way" because it served as a sort of bridge between the Protestants (Lutherans and Reformed) and the Roman Church (the Roman Church being those churches under the authority of the Bishop of Rome, the Pope).

John and Charles Wesley were priests in the Church of England. During their lives the appointment of clergy to parishes became highly political, and the ministry suffered from chronic neglect and apathy. Many of the clergymen were absentee leaders. It was a common practice for a priest to live a comfortable life in London while he paid a minister to carry out his pastoral duties in the parish to which he was appointed. Consequently, the needs of the people in the parish often were neglected. Few attended worship services; fewer still received the sacrament of the Lord's Supper on the Sundays it was offered. The church made little effort to minister to the needs of the ordinary people, most of whom were poor. The church carried out its ceremonial functions for the royal family and Parliament, but it had little impact or importance in the daily lives of most of its members and priests. While there certainly were vital parishes scattered throughout England, the Anglican Church of the eighteenth century was, for the most part, a hollow institution.

The established church's neglect of the vast majority of people contributed to the rise of an Evangelical revival that swept across Britain through much of the eighteenth century. The support structure of the revival was a network of religious societies, such as the Society for the Propagation of the Gospel (S.P.G.) and the Society for Promoting Christian Knowledge (S.P.C.K.), which were primarily missionary societies that sought to spread the good news of Jesus Christ to all people through religious education and evangelism. Much of their work was directed abroad in the various British colonies, especially in America. There were smaller societies that held regular meetings that included the reading and study of Scripture, preaching, prayer, and hymn singing. These societies existed to help ordinary people live as disciples of Jesus Christ. Key leaders who emerged from these societies were George Whitefield and John and Charles Wesley.

John Wesley

On June 17, 1703, John Wesley was born into the large family of Susanna and Samuel Wesley. Samuel Wesley was the rector (priest) of the parish of Epworth, England. The Wesleys lived a hard life as the parsonage family in a town that viewed the established church with disdain and suspicion. The tension between the church and many of the Epworth citizens became so difficult at times that the rectory (parsonage) was burned on two occasions. Arson was suspected. The second of those fires had a profound impact on the life of John Wesley, who was five years old and the last of the children to be saved from the flames. From that time on his mother referred to him as "a brand plucked out of the burning" because she believed that God had saved her son for a divine purpose.

Their father often was away from home or busy with parish affairs, so Susanna was the dominant and most influential of John's parents. She was a strong and disciplined leader of the household and also earned a reputation as a leader in the Epworth parish. In fact, many preferred her leadership and skill as a teacher to her husband's, which caused some friction within the rectory. Susanna would lead Bible study sessions in the kitchen. Often, they overflowed the room into the yard, so people in the yard listened through the open windows. John and Charles were deeply influenced by their mother's abiding love for God and neighbors.

Each week Susanna would spend an hour with each of her children. This time was special for the children because it was when they could count on receiving their mother's undivided attention. Susanna used this time to learn the state of the child's spiritual and emotional well-being. It also was a time for one-with-one religious instruction. This weekly time with his mother was precious to John, and it had a profound impact on the whole of his life. Susanna was his spiritual mentor, and her disciplined and loving hand can be seen in his life and ministry.

John was educated at Charterhouse school in London and at Christ Church College, Oxford. While at Oxford, he and his brother Charles led a group of devout fellow students that became known variously as the Holy Club, Bible Moths, and Methodists. They were dedicated to regular devotions, good works, and visiting prisoners. During his time at Oxford, John Wesley began to take seriously his life as a Christian. He sought to form himself into a Christian through a rigorous discipline of study, prayer, good works, and accountability with the Holy Club. During this period he began to keep a detailed journal of his thoughts and actions. With the encouragement of his mother, and especially of his father, John focused his studies at Oxford on ordination as a priest for the Church of England. In 1726, he was elected a fellow of Lincoln College, Oxford. The fellowship provided him the security of regular income, responsibility for tutoring students, and access at least once a year to the pulpit at St. Mary's Church, the university's church. The income from the fellowship eventually freed Wesley to travel and preach in the countryside and towns across England. In 1728, John Wesley was ordained a priest. In 1726 and 1729, he served as his father's assistant at Epworth and Wroot.

In 1735, shortly after their father's death, both John and Charles accepted invitations to serve in the colony of Georgia in America. With the help of the Society for the Propagation of the Gospel, John would serve as priest for the colonists and missionary to the Indians. Charles would serve as the governor's secretary for Indian affairs. At this point in his life, John was experiencing increasing disillusionment with the work at Oxford, especially with the struggling Methodist society. He saw the opportunity to serve as a voluntary missionary in Georgia as a way to the salvation of his soul. Wesley had hoped that whatever God had in store for him in the colony would give him an opportunity to do more good for Christ's sake and for his own.

On the voyage to America, John was assigned to be the ship's chaplain. On board was a group of Moravians, a German-speaking people known for their piety. The voyage was difficult, as the ship was battered by several storms. One particularly severe storm caused a great deal of damage to the ship. It was during that storm that Wesley was most impressed by the faith of the Moravians. While he sat in his cabin fearing for his life, he heard the Moravians singing hymns and praying for themselves and the ship's company. While chaos was all about them, their faith in God calmed them and allowed them to weather the storm. It was this deep and abiding faith Wesley sought for himself, so he determined to get to know the Moravians after that night.

Wesley's experience in Georgia added to his disillusionment. He soon discovered that the colonists were not interested in his ministry, and that many had gone to Georgia to escape the church and its clergy. They were independent-minded frontier folk who had little time for authority of any kind, least of all priests. And the Indians Wesley had so looked forward to evangelizing were equally unimpressed with him.

Wesley's tenure in Georgia was brought to an unfortunate end by a failed love affair. It is believed that Sophy Hopkey had won John's heart. They shared each other's company to such an extent that people began to talk about them. The relationship, for reasons no one really knows, came to an abrupt end and Sophy married a Mr. Williamson. Wesley was deeply wounded by these events, which contributed to a deepening in his personal and spiritual disillusionment and caused him to question his faith in God and the salvation of his soul. He responded by spurning Sophy in public and refusing to serve her the Lord's Supper. The latter deeply offended her husband and uncle, a prominent shopkeeper and a magistrate, who brought charges against Wesley. In December 1737, Wesley boarded a ship and headed home to England, never to see America again. He left with a cloud of scandal over his head at what was, no doubt, the lowest point of his life.

The one truly positive aspect of the Georgia experience was the relationship Wesley formed with the Moravians, whose piety and evangelical fervor appealed to Wesley. They would prove to be an important factor in the rest of his life. In February 1738, soon after he returned to London, Wesley met a young Moravian pastor named Peter Böhler, whose conversations were a great source of comfort, challenge, and encouragement. It was Böhler who helped him develop his understanding of justification (restored relationship with God) by grace through faith.

Aldersgate Street

On May 24, 1738, Wesley was still recovering from his disastrous experience in Georgia when some friends convinced him to attend a meeting of a Moravian society at Aldersgate Street in London. That evening something happened that had a profound impact on John Wesley's life and marked the beginning of what would become the Methodist revival. He recorded the event in his journal that night in these famous words:

> In the evening I went very unwillingly to a society in Aldersgate Street, where one was reading Luther's Preface to the Epistle to the Romans. About a quarter before nine, while he was describing the change which God works in the heart through faith in Christ, I felt my heart strangely

warmed. I felt I did trust in Christ, Christ alone for salvation, and an assurance was given me that he had taken away *my* sins, even *mine,* and saved *me* from the law of sin and death.

(From *The Works of John Wesley,* Volume 18, edited by W. Reginald Ward and Richard P. Heitzenrater, pages 249–50. © 1988 Abingdon Press. Used by permission.)

At Aldersgate Street Wesley received the assurance of salvation he had sought for so long. He got the order of salvation right that night. Up until then he had been striving for a right relationship with God through living a holy life, practicing spiritual disciplines, and doing good works. But at that Aldersgate meeting house he finally understood that his relationship with God had already been restored by Jesus Christ, and Christ alone. The hard work of reconciliation had been done at the cross and the empty tomb. There was nothing neither he nor anyone could do. God had done it all for the world and for him in Christ, crucified and risen. Wesley's heart was filled with a peace and joy that had been absent for a long time.

Soon after his experience at Aldersgate Street, Wesley, filled with a new zeal born of his experience of assurance, traveled to Germany where he visited the headquarters of the Moravians. Count von Zinzendorf had created a Moravian community on his estate known as Herrnhut. Wesley went there in order to learn more about how the Moravians lived out their faith in Christ. He observed their community life, attended their worship services, interviewed members and leaders (including Zinzendorf), and traveled the surrounding countryside during the three months he lived among the Moravians. While listening to their sermons and engaging them in theological discussions, Wesley learned much that helped him clarify his own experience in theological terms. They especially helped him understand more clearly the doctrine that was to become the centerpiece of his preaching: justification by grace through faith.

Wesley also closely observed the organization of the Herrnhut community, which was divided into choirs and small groups known as classes and bands. The choirs were large groups that were divided into classes, which were geographic groupings. The classes in turn were divided into smaller, more-intimate bands. The purpose of the groupings was to provide the members with communal support, nurture, discipline, and accountability. The Moravian organizational structures made a significant impression on Wesley.

He returned to England in September 1738. During the autumn and winter of that year, Wesley continued to struggle with and test his faith. As was his manner, he engaged in serious study and self-examination. He read the writings of Jonathan Edwards, the famous American preacher and theologian. Edwards was the leader in the American colonies of the Evangelical revival known as the Great Awakening, which began in New England in 1734. Edwards' preaching on the need for a personal experience and conversion to Christ were of particular interest to Wesley as he sought to understand his own experience and how to convey it to the world. He also rediscovered the homilies, a collection of historic sermons that contained the doctrinal teachings of the Church of England. The months of study, self-examination, and preaching in churches around London helped prepare Wesley for the next pivotal decision of his life.

Revival

George Whitefield was a gifted preacher and a member of the original Oxford Holy Club with John and Charles Wesley. He had followed the Wesleys to Georgia, where he established an orphanage. Upon his return to England in 1738, Whitefield began preaching at churches in and around Bristol. His preaching had a profound influence on a large number of people. Many of the local rectors did not appreciate the response, so Whitefield was banned from most pulpits. This did not stop Rev. George Whitefield, who then began the practice of open-air preaching. There are reports of thousands of people at a time coming to hear Whitefield's preaching in the fields and squares of Bristol. As he was preparing to head west to preach in Wales, Whitefield wrote to John Wesley inviting him to come and take over where he was about to leave off.

Whitefield was a powerful orator, and he knew how to present the gospel in a way that touched and moved people to receive Christ into their hearts. Because of his skill as a preacher, Whitefield often attracted hundreds, and sometimes thousands, of people when he preached in public squares and in open fields. However, he did not have the organizational skills needed to sustain a revival. So when it was time for him to leave Bristol, he called on his friend and colleague John Wesley to come to Bristol and give growth to the seeds he had planted.

Wesley went to Bristol reluctantly because he had reservations about open-air preaching. As a devout churchman, Wesley was suspicious of such unorthodox methods. He consulted with friends and spent much time in prayer. He also studied the Scriptures. It was his study of the Sermon on the Mount (Matthew 5–7) that helped convince him that field preaching was acceptable to God. After all, Jesus had done it himself. Wesley wrote in his journal after his first field sermon that he "submitted to be more vile." In other words, Wesley determined, after much discernment, that God was calling him to move beyond the conventions of the church to reach those people whom the church had neglected. On April 2, 1739, he preached his first open-air sermon to three thousand people in a brick field near Bristol. His text was Luke 4:18-19:

> The Spirit of the Lord is upon me,
>   because he has anointed me
>   to bring good news to the poor.
> He has sent me to proclaim release
>   to the captives
>   and recovery of sight to the blind,
>   to let the oppressed go free,
> to proclaim the year of the Lord's favor.

John Wesley's life, and the lives of many who heard him that day, was changed forever.

Class Meetings: The Method of Methodism

Wesley saw as God's affirmation of his decision the large numbers of people who gathered in the fields to hear him preach and the way many of them responded. He gained a new confidence in himself and in the faith God had given him at Aldersgate Street. He believed that the message of forgiveness of sin and salvation by grace through faith alone was indeed good news to the poor and working people of Bristol and London. Many who heard Wesley experienced forgiveness for their sins and a desire to live their lives anew with Christ at the center. They, in turn, joined the religious societies that met in Bristol and London. Consequently, those societies experienced a dramatic increase in membership and attendance. At this early point in the revival, the societies were not Methodist in identity. Wesley associated with and provided spiritual leadership for several societies, but he was most closely associated with the Fetter Lane Society in London.

Eventually, several Bristol and London religious societies that were related to the Church of England came under the leadership and control of John Wesley. Two of the Bristol societies grew to a point where they required more space for their meetings, so they agreed to unite in the building of a new meeting house that eventually became known as the New Room. Likewise, Wesley worked to acquire the site of an old cannon foundry in London that could be renovated and used as a Methodist meeting house. This building became known simply as the Foundry.

These societies consisted of people who, in Wesley's words, sought to "flee from the wrath to come." In other words, these early Methodists were women and men who had experienced conviction and forgiveness of their sins and wanted to claim their new life in Christ. They came to the society to learn more about their newfound faith and how to live it out in the world. Some of the people also were in small groups known as bands, whose purpose was spiritual growth through confession and prayer. The bands provided an intimate setting for accountability and support for growing in faith. To help build the intimacy of the groups, the bands were self-selecting and homogeneous (men meeting with men, and women meeting with women). The size of the bands was from five to ten people. Not everyone in a society was in a band, but everyone in the bands was a member of the society. The bands were similar to the Moravian groups Wesley observed at Herrnhut, but they were not an exact replica. The primary difference was in their emphasis on spiritual growth through mutual accountability, confession, and Christian conversation. The Moravian bands, which were more hierarchical, were under a leader who monitored the spiritual progress of each member. The Wesleyan bands were a reflection of Wesley's understanding of justification and sanctification, which was different from that of the Moravians. He believed that there were degrees of faith, and that justification was not a once-and-forever change. It was a daily, ongoing concern that enabled the person to struggle with doubts and fears and, ultimately, to grow in grace, faith, and love for God and neighbor. The purpose of the bands was to support such struggle and growth in the believer's daily life.

Because of growing theological differences between Wesley and the Moravians in the Fetter Lane Society, he and many of his followers moved on July 23, 1740, to the society meeting at the Foundry. At this point, the Foundry society began to flourish, while the Fetter Lane society, torn by internal conflict and without Wesley's leadership skills, eventually disbanded.

The various societies associated with Wesley continued to grow, as did the debt incurred for the building of the New Room in Bristol. Something needed to be done to retire the debt, because it was becoming too great for Wesley, who had taken the debt on himself. The problem faced by the societies was that the vast majority of members were poor and could not afford to contribute. On February 15, 1742, Wesley called a meeting with leaders of the respective societies to find a way to retire the building debts.

It was suggested that each member be asked to contribute a penny a week. However, some opposed this plan because many of the society members could not afford that amount. This led to the idea of dividing the societies into small groups of twelve known as classes. Each class would have an identified leader, who would be responsible for collecting the contributions. The class leader would visit the members once a week and be responsible for turning in twelve pennies at the end of the week. The class leaders would make up any shortfall that occurred when poor members were not able to contribute. This plan, which was agreed to by Wesley and the society leaders, was the genesis of the Methodist class meeting.

The classes were different from the bands. Classes, consisting of up to twelve and sometimes as many as twenty people, tended to be larger in size than the bands. All society members were assigned to a class, which included both men and women. They were not self-selecting. People were assigned to classes based on geography, by neighborhood or district. Each class had an assigned leader who was selected by Wesley. The content of the class meeting was less intimate and intense than the band meeting, and the focus was on the pastoral and instructional more than on mutual accountability. While the bands were collegial in nature, the classes were more leader oriented.

As the leaders gave their weekly reports to Wesley, he soon realized the pastoral potential of the classes and class leaders. He thought that the class meetings were more conducive to the lives of working people than were the bands. The work of the leaders, as they visited and looked after their class members, extended the pastoral ministry of the societies to all members. Soon after its inception, the classes became much more than a means for retiring a building debt; they became the very foundation on which the Methodist movement was built. The class meeting provided the means for spiritual nurture and accountability sought by those who came to join the Methodist societies.

In the early days of the classes, the leaders were expected to visit each week with each member of his or her class. These individual visits were time-consuming for the leaders, so many did not have time to get to every member by the end of each week. Therefore, someone suggested that the class assemble with the leader once a week. This assembly became the class meeting.

What happened in these class meetings? After everyone had assembled, the leader would open the meeting with a prayer and a few stanzas of a hymn. He or she would then proceed to give an accounting of his or her life since the last meeting. The leader always began the process of telling the story of his or her struggles, triumphs, joys, and concerns with regard to the state of his or her soul and relationship with Christ. The purpose of this accounting was twofold: First, it unburdened the leader. Second, and more importantly, it helped the class members understand that they were not alone in their struggles and doubts. The accounting was not to be self-centered; it was to be done in a way that was instructive for the class.

After the leader finished giving his or her account, he or she would turn to a member of the class and ask, "Well, sister (or brother), how do you find the state of your soul this evening?" That person would then unburden him or herself to the leader. This process would be repeated until every member of the class had been given an opportunity to talk. The dynamic of these exchanges was always a question-answer format facilitated by the class leader. After all the members had been given the opportunity to give an account of the week, the leader concluded the meeting with a time of prayer. He or she began with an extemporaneous prayer and then asked that those members who felt led by the Holy Spirit to offer prayers. The prayers continued until the leader brought the meeting to a close with the singing of a hymn. Then the class was dismissed for the week.

Another dynamic of the class meetings was the relationships formed between the class leaders and the members of the class and between the class members themselves. As the classes met each week and the members shared their burdens with one another, they inevitably grew in their love for one another. Over time, trust was built that enabled deeper and deeper levels of sharing and accountability. The class members came to "watch over one another in love." The love and trust for one another and the discipline of weekly accountability provided an environment for growth in faith. The closer people are drawn to God, the closer they come to their neighbor. The class meeting provided an environment in which people could trust and be trusted, love and be loved, and be vulnerable in a way that is needed for true growth in grace and love of God, neighbor, and self to occur.

The only condition for membership in a Methodist society was "a desire to flee from the wrath to come, and to be saved from their sins." (From "A Plain Account of the People Called Methodists," in *The Works of John Wesley*, Volume 9, edited by Rupert E. Davies, page 257. © 1989 Abingdon Press. Used by permission.) The condition to remain a member was participation in the weekly class meeting. Each member of the society eventually was issued a ticket, which was a sign of membership in the society and was renewed quarterly based on regular attendance in the weekly class meeting. If a member frequently was absent or habitually disregarded the General Rules of the United Societies, his or her ticket would be revoked and he or she would be excluded from membership in the society. All that was required for reinstatement was an expression of repentance and intention to keep the General Rules.

What were the General Rules? They were the household rules for the Methodist societies. The General Rules were not rules in the sense of being laws; rather, they were like a rule that, when placed on a piece of paper, helps you draw a straight line. They were standards for living that directed people in the way of Jesus Christ. They were like the needle on a compass that showed the way to go and prevented people from getting lost. The rules were general in the sense that they involved the whole of a person's life, just as Christ and his grace address the whole human being. The more one made the General Rules a part of daily life, the more he or she could be formed into the image of Christ.

The General Rules were (and are) simple and straightforward:

4. There is one only condition previously required in those who desire admission into these societies, "a desire to flee from the wrath to come, to be saved from their sins." But wherever this is really fixed in the soul it will be shown by its fruits. It is therefore expected of all who continue therein that they should continue to evidence their desire of salvation,

First, By doing no harm, by avoiding evil in every kind—especially that which is most generally practised. Such is:

The taking the name of God in vain.

The profaning the day of the Lord, either by doing ordinary work thereon, or by buying or selling.

Drunkenness, *buying or selling spirituous liquors;* or *drinking them* (unless in cases of extreme necessity).

Fighting, quarrelling, brawling; brother "going to law" with brother; returning evil for evil, or railing for railing; the "using many words" in buying or selling.

The *buying or selling uncustomed goods.*

The *giving or taking things on usury.*

Uncharitable or *unprofitable* conversation, especially *speaking evil of ministers or those in authority.*

Doing to others as we would not they should do unto us.

Doing what we know is not for the glory of God, as,

The "putting on of gold or costly apparel,"…

The *taking such diversions* as cannot be used in the name of the Lord Jesus,

The *singing* those *songs,* or *reading* those *books,* which do not tend to the knowledge or love of God;

Softness, and needless self-indulgence;

Laying up treasures upon earth;

Borrowing without a probability of paying: or taking up goods without a probability of paying for them.

5. It is expected of all who continue in these societies that they should continue to evidence their desire of salvation,

Secondly, By doing good, by being in every kind merciful after their power, as they have opportunity doing good of every possible sort and as far as is possible to all men:

To their bodies, of the ability which God giveth, by giving food to the hungry, by clothing the naked, by visiting or helping them that are sick, or in prison.

To their souls, by instructing, *reproving,* or exhorting all they have any intercourse with; trampling under foot that enthusiastic doctrine of devils, that "we are not to do good unless *our heart be free to it.*"

By doing good especially to them that are of the household of faith, or groaning so to be; employing them preferably to others, buying one of another, helping each other in business—and that so much the more because the world will love its own, and them only.

By all possible *diligence* and *frugality,* that the gospel be not blamed.

By running with patience the race that is set before them; "denying themselves, and taking up their cross daily"; submitting to bear the reproach of Christ, to be as the filth and offscouring of the world; and looking that men should "say all manner of evil of them falsely, for the Lord's sake."

6. It is expected of all who desire to continue in these societies that they should continue to evidence their desire of salvation,

Thirdly, By attending upon all the ordinances of God. Such are:

The public worship of God;

The ministry of the Word, either read or expounded;

The Supper of the Lord;

Family and private prayer;

Searching the Scriptures; and

Fasting, or abstinence.

(From "The Nature, Design, and General Rules of the United Societies," in *The Works of John Wesley,* Volume 9, edited by Rupert E. Davies, pages 70–73. © 1989 Abingdon Press. Used by permission.)

While some of the prohibitions mentioned may seem quaint or irrelevant to us today, they addressed real dangers and social problems faced by the people of Wesley's day. If you take time to examine them closely, I am certain you will be able to find contemporary temptations and distractions that parallel those of the early Methodists.

The emphasis of the General Rules was an acknowledgment of the human need for divine grace and a desire to live a life that is a reflection of the grace that was revealed to the world in the life, death, and resurrection of Jesus Christ. The rules provided a concrete, practical guide for how to live out God's household rules (see Chapter 2) contained in the Ten Commandments and summarized by Jesus in the Great Commandment (Matthew 22:34-40). Wesley believed that God, by grace, has provided means that give people access to this grace. Doing, and not doing, specific actions made people more available to God than they would be otherwise. These actions are known as means of grace (see Chapter 3).

The General Rules provided the framework for the weekly class meetings and were the guidelines for the telling of their lives since they last met. The class leaders and members told one another what they did and did not do. The rules served as their compass; the weekly class meeting, with the giving account and sharing of prayer, provided their compass heading. It helped them know where they stood and gave them an indicator of where they were headed. The class meeting also gave people an opportunity to make needed course corrections. The General Rules helped give guidance for living as disciples of Jesus Christ in the world by providing needed boundaries. Like a loving parent sets boundaries for a child's behavior that reflect the values of the family, the General Rules were a reflection of the values of the branch of God's household known as the Methodists.

The General Rules continue to be part of The United Methodist Church today. You can find them in Part II of *The Book of Discipline of The United Methodist Church.* Two of the historic questions asked of candidates for ordination as an elder in The United Methodist Church are, "Do you know the General Rules of our church?" and "Will you keep them?" Today, the General Rule of Discipleship restates the General Rules in contemporary language. It states that those who desire to live as Christian disciples will covenant to witness to Jesus Christ in the world and follow his teachings through acts of compassion, justice, worship, and devotion under the guidance of the Holy Spirit. The General Rule of Discipleship provides a framework to guide the life of Covenant Discipleship Groups, just as the General Rules did for the early class meetings. It also provides a means for people to live out God's household rules and become a channel of grace for others in their daily lives.

The class meeting became the muscle of the Methodist movement in England and America. From it emerged leaders who became mentors and lay pastors for countless men, women, children, and families. People were brought to saving faith in Christ, and their faith was nurtured and lived. People who lived hard lives in grinding poverty in a world that regarded them as nothing more than a beast of burden found a place where they were somebody, a brother or sister in Christ and fellow sojourner in the faith. The class meeting gave many meaning and purpose for lives that otherwise were bleak and empty. In the weekly time of praying, hymn singing, and telling their story (accountability), they found in their class people who called them by name and listened.

The class leader was the mentor many needed to nurture, challenge, and correct them along the way. The class meeting was the means by which the Methodists lived out the commandments of Christ. They brought good news to the poor, proclaimed release to the captives, recovery of sight to the blind, set free the oppressed, fed the hungry, clothed the naked, welcomed the stranger, and visited the sick and the prisoners. Through the class meeting the Methodists were nurtured in their faith and were given the grace they needed to love God, to love their neighbor as they loved themselves, and to love one another as Christ loved them. The class meeting was the engine that moved the Methodists forward. Grace was the fuel that provided the power.

Conclusion

John Wesley was many things in his life. He was a preacher's kid, a student and scholar, a tutor and teacher, an organizer, and a preacher, but most of all he was a pastor. His greatest concern was for people and their physical and spiritual welfare. Wesley referred to himself as "a man of one book" (the Bible), which meant that he was a lifelong student of the Bible. He took it seriously as divine revelation to humankind. It was the church's book through which human beings could come to saving knowledge of God and God's action for humankind and all creation in Jesus Christ. Wesley also drank deeply of the writings of the early church (first through third century) and of the Eastern (Orthodox) fathers. He was a student of the history, tradition, and theologies of the church.

Wesley was a dedicated churchman who lived and died a loyal priest of the Church of England. The mission of the Methodist movement, as he saw it, was "to reform the nation, particularly the Church; and to spread scriptural holiness over the land." (From "Minutes of Several Conversations Between the Rev. Mr. Wesley and Others, From the Year 1744, to the Year 1789," by John Wesley.) Wesley saw the Methodist revival as an opportunity for his beloved Church of England to renew its commitment to Christ by serving Christ in the world. He also saw the church's neglect of the poor and working folk of England and its passive silence in the face of the injustice of slavery and war. His pastor's heart ached for those voiceless people in whom he saw the face of the Savior of the world.

Wesley was a man who struggled with doubt and often questioned his faith. He was not afraid to engage God in expressing his anguish over his identity as a Christian. While Wesley expressed doubts in himself and his relationship with God, he never questioned God's love and grace for him and for all people. Wesley was in all respects an honest man with his neighbor, with himself, and with his God. He did not fear the truth. In fact, it could be argued that his whole life was a quest and struggle for knowing and living the truth, made human in Jesus Christ (John 8:32; 14:6).

Wesley was a man who would not be limited by convention or tradition. He trusted his experience and pastoral instincts enough to be willing to try new ideas. If they worked, he kept at them; if not, he let them go and moved on. In this regard, Wesley always was open to the leading of the Holy Spirit in his life and in the revival that became the Methodist movement. He was not afraid to listen to and learn from people whose voices more conventional priests would likely be inclined to ignore. The best example of this is Wesley's relationship with the Moravians, whose pietist tradition was different from the more-formal piety of the Church of England. Wesley saw in them a spirit of love, patience, joy, and courage that he wanted for himself, so he listened and learned from them. He took from the Moravians elements of their theology and organization that could be adapted and applied to his setting. Wesley was practical and, at times, pragmatic. He tended to go with what worked for him and for the people who followed him.

The class meetings were probably the most important result of Wesley's willingness to listen, learn, adapt, and implement new ideas. While the class meeting model was hardly a new idea—it has its origins in the primitive church—it was new to the Methodists. Because Wesley followed the prompting of the Holy Spirit and implemented the division of the societies into classes, he discovered and set loose the power of God to change lives and care for people's bodies and souls.

Wesley was a pastor's pastor. We can see this in his embrace of the class meetings and the office of class leader. Through them, the pastoral needs of countless people were met, and they were loved and formed into Christian disciples. They experienced the forgiveness of their sins and, often for the first time, learned that they were somebody in the eyes of God and their neighbor. We can look to Wesley and those early class meetings and learn from them as we seek to raise up faithful disciples and leaders in the church of today.

Covenant Discipleship Groups, which are direct descendants of the class meetings of so long ago, are the result of some of our learning. Their mission is to form Christian disciples through mutual support and accountability. Wesley would be pleased to see Covenant Discipleship Groups because they address the pastoral concern for reaching people with the love of God and forming leaders who are equipped to help others grow in faith and love for God and their neighbor.

For Reflection and Discussion

1. Look at the General Rules (pages 94–95) and notice the list of evils to avoid under the first rule: "By doing no harm, by avoiding evil in every kind." Which of the evils listed there still apply to life in today's world? What, do you think, could be added to update the list for today?
2. Reflect on your family history. What does it tell you about yourself? How does your history influence the person you are today? How does your history determine the person you may become?
3. John Wesley was not afraid to look at a variety of traditions and draw on them for his own ministry. Given today's world, which groups or movements of today do you think Wesley would look to for ideas for improving the ministry and mission of The United Methodist Church?
4. How is the world of eighteenth-century England similar to the world of today? How is it different?
5. Can you identify a time when you had an experience similar to Wesley's at Aldersgate Street on May 24, 1738? What happened? How were you changed?
6. If today's United Methodist preachers were to emulate George Whitefield and John Wesley when they preached in the open air, where would they go? Do you think many would stop to listen to what they had to say?

To Learn More

Reasonable Enthusiast: John Wesley and the Rise of Methodism, by Henry D. Rack (Nashville: Abingdon Press, 1993).

Wesley and the People Called Methodists, by Richard P. Heitzenrater (Nashville: Abingdon Press, 1995).

Class Leaders: Stewards of Sanctification

The men and women known as class leaders formed the backbone of the Methodist movement for 250 years. They were people with the experience of justifying faith that equipped them for ministry among their peers. Class leaders provided the pastoral care and leadership for the early Methodist societies while the preachers were riding their circuits. They were the glue that held the Methodist movement together and gave it the strength and cohesiveness that enabled it to transform countless lives.

This chapter will explore the ministry of the class leaders, who they were, what they did, and why they were so important to the Methodist movement. First, we will focus our attention on a brief account of the rise of class leaders in the Wesleyan revival. Next, we will look at the biblical foundation and rationale for the office of class leader. Then, we will examine the theological necessity for discipleship leadership. Finally, we will explore briefly the need to recover the office of class leader within the contemporary United Methodist Church.

How Class Leaders Came to Be

John Wesley was blessed by God with many gifts for ministry, one of which was an extraordinary skill for organization. His understanding of salvation led him to develop an organization that was a means of grace. In other words, class members were given the instruction, support, accountability, and communal love needed to help them experience and grow in their faith and love of God and neighbor. They experienced the love of Christ through their class leader and fellow class members as they grew in love and trust with one another.

Wesley also understood the importance of structure and order for the success of any human endeavor. He worked hard to give the people who responded to the good news of grace in Jesus Christ the structure needed for their emerging faith to grow and mature. He used his experience of Anglican and Moravian religious societies to guide his thinking as he organized the people called Methodists for ministry.

Wesley and the Methodists developed a structure that supported people. It was a means of grace because its purpose was to give people a place where they could receive support and encouragement for their faith in Christ. It instructed them in the basics of Christian faith and provided the support and accountability needed for them to live out their faith in the world of family and work. Within the Methodist societies, people experienced prevenient, justifying, and sanctifying grace. The purpose of the structure was to support the people in their discipleship, to help them "lead a life worthy of the calling to which [they were] called" (Ephesians 4:1).

The class meeting was the building block of the Methodist structure. Wesley describes how he and other Methodist leaders chanced upon the idea:

> At length, while we were thinking of quite another thing, we struck upon a method for which we have cause to bless God ever since. I was talking with several of the society in Bristol concerning the means of paying the debts there, when one stood up and said, "Let every member of the society give a *penny* a week till all are paid." Another answered, "But many of them are poor, and cannot afford to do it." "Then," said he, "put eleven of the poorest with me, and if they can give anything, well. I will call on them weekly, and if they can give nothing, I will give for them as well as for myself. And each of you, call on eleven of your neighbours weekly; receive what they give, and make up what is wanting." It was done. In a while some of these informed me, they found such and such an one did not live as he ought. It struck me immediately. "This is the thing, the very thing we have wanted so long." I called together all the *Leaders* of the *Classes* (so we used to term them and their

companies), and desired that each would make a particular inquiry into the behaviour of those whom he saw weekly. They did so. Many disorderly walkers were detected. Some turned from the evil of their ways. Some were put away from us. Many saw it with fear, and rejoiced unto God with reverence.

(From "A Plain Account of the People Called Methodists," in *The Works of John Wesley,* Volume 9, edited by Rupert E. Davies, pages 260–61. © 1989 Abingdon Press. Used by permission.)

This became the pattern for all the Methodist societies. The need to retire a building debt led to an important organizational step forward for the Wesleyan movement. Wesley soon saw the potential for ordering the Methodist societies into classes under the leadership of class leaders, who provided the pastoral care and guidance needed to nurture the people in their faith and discipleship. The classes became a locus for Christian formation.

At first Wesley instructed the leaders to visit with their class members individually in their homes or places of work. They soon realized this practice consumed far too much of the leaders' time and energy. To resolve the problem of overextended leaders, Wesley ordered the leaders to assemble their classes for weekly meetings. In the weekly class meeting, the leader and the class prayed, sang hymns, read and discussed the Scriptures, and gave an account of their lives since the last meeting. The class meeting was a time for mutual sharing, support, and accountability. Attendance at the meetings was a requirement of membership in the society because it was the glue that held the society and its members together with Christ. The class meeting was where people "watched over one another in love."

By the standards of today, the class meetings probably seem rigid and exclusive, and to a degree they were. But we need to remember that everyone entering a Methodist society understood that participation in a class was expected. If a person did not want to submit to the discipline of the class and the class leader, then he or she was not ready to be part of a Methodist society. However, these people remained members of the Anglican Church. Their membership or lack of membership in a Methodist society did not affect their church membership. We also need to know that the discipline and accountability experienced in the class meeting was not intended to be judgmental or harsh. It was done in the spirit of love. The leader, who was not in any way exempt from the accountability, was always the first to give an account. In fact, as seasoned Christians and role models, the leaders were held to a higher standard than were their class members. The discipline of the class was born of love and a desire and expectation that the members sought to grow in grace, that they were moving forward in their sanctification and going on to perfection (maturity) in love. When members were dismissed for lack of attendance, for drunkenness, for not keeping the General Rules (see Chapter 4), or for any other reason, it was always with the understanding that they would be welcome back when they were ready to live by the General Rules and had given evidence of such readiness. The class meeting was indeed rigid in the sense that it placed expectations on its members. The expectations were that they ought to live as disciples of Jesus Christ and would do all in their power to live out their discipleship according to Jesus' commands to love God and love their neighbor as themselves. And the classes were exclusive in that membership was limited to those who showed consistent evidence of a desire to live as disciples in the world. But we must remember that the discipline and accountability were viewed as means to grow in justifying and sanctifying grace (see Chapter 3). They worked together to build the people up and help them along the way of salvation toward Christian perfection.

Class Leaders

Who were these class leaders? They were men and women whom Wesley believed exhibited maturity in Christian faith and love. They also displayed leadership abilities and a desire to serve Christ. They came from all walks of life, and most were working people of modest means. The one thing they had in common was faith in God and God's Son, Jesus Christ. Their faith led them to desire to walk with him and to serve him in the world. They responded to saving grace by seeking the mind of Christ and by working out their own salvation (Philippians 2:12). The class leaders were women and men who committed themselves to working out their faith through love (Galatians 5:6) by loving God with all their heart, soul, mind, and strength and loving their neighbor as themselves. They sought to please God by helping others to know and to claim the salvation that had been won for them by Jesus Christ, crucified and risen.

In *The Class-Leader's Manual* (New York: Carlton & Phillips, 1852; pages 152–79), Rev. Charles C. Keys describes the qualifications of a class leader:

1. This office should not be assumed hastily, and without serious premeditation....
2. It is necessary that the class-leader[s] should understand [their] position; that [they] should be acquainted with the nature and responsibilities of [their] office, and that from voluntary choice [they] should bear this burden....

3. The leader should be a [person] of some business talent. System and punctuality are required of [him or her] in attending the interests of [the] class, as well as in performing with acceptability and profit the other duties of [the] station....
4. Leaders should be [people] of sound judgment. They should have some discernment of character, and a knowledge of human nature, and be able to determine on the most judicious means for reaching all the ends of their appointment....
5. This officer should also have some talent for speaking—some gift of exhortation and prayer....
6. While thus endeavouring to acquire the talent of speaking in public, you are subjecting your mind to discipline and cultivation, and at the same time enlarging your stock of religious knowledge....
7. A class-leader should be known as a true Methodist....
8. "But, above all, this office should be filled by [people] "truly devoted to God."

Keys goes on to say about class leaders:

However superior your other gifts and endowments may be, if you have not piety, you are unfit to be a leader among us; your example will not edify, whatever your words may do; the duties of your office will be irksome, and often neglected, or carelessly performed; and you will at last be unprepared to give up your account to the great Head of the Church.

Leaders were expected to be models of Christian character for the society and their class. They were men and women who had experienced justification and the new birth. Christ was at the center of their lives. They took to heart and applied, as best they could, to their daily lives Jesus' commands to love God, neighbor, and self.

Now that we know who class leaders were and the expectations and qualifications imposed on them, we need to look at what they did. For this we go to Wesley himself:

1. To see each person in his class once a week at the least; in order
   To inquire how their souls prosper;
   To advise, reprove, comfort, or exhort, as occasion may require.
   To receive what they are willing to give toward the relief of the poor.
2. To meet the Minister and the stewards of the Society in order:
   To inform the minister of any that are sick, or of any that are disorderly and will not be reproved.
   To pay to the stewards what they have received of their several classes in the week preceding.

(From "A Plain Account of the People Called Methodists," in *The Works of John Wesley*, Volume 9, edited by Rupert E. Davies, page 261. © 1989 Abingdon Press. Used by permission.)

We can see here that class leaders had no small task. They were essentially lay pastors who were given pastoral responsibility for the members of their class, which was as many as twelve people and sometimes more. The leader's first responsibility was to meet with members of the class weekly to provide spiritual care and instruction. Leaders needed to have some maturity and experience in faith and discipleship in order to discern the needs of each person and to give appropriate care. In their ministry of inquiring how the souls of their charges prospered, the leaders gave them weekly opportunity to give an account of how they had kept or had not kept the General Rules (doing no harm, doing good, and attending to the means of instituted means of grace). This helped class members more clearly understand their own spiritual state and gave them a healthy compass heading for the week to come. As the leader gave class members an opportunity to tell about the state of their life with Christ, he or she offered advice, chastised those who had committed sins or who chronically had failed to keep the General Rules, comforted those in distress, and gave instruction in the faith to those who needed help and encouragement. We can see from the depth of responsibility borne by the class leaders why the qualifications were so demanding. This was not an office entered into lightly. The leaders were given responsibility for the spiritual well-being of their sisters and brothers in Christ.

This is why the second part of their job description was necessary. The class leaders needed to be accountable to the minister and steward of the society, so they met monthly along with the other leaders to give an accounting of the spiritual well-being of their class. This gave the minister an opportunity to discern the spiritual and physical state not only of each class but also of each class leader. The leaders were responsible for keeping the minister, who was given charge of a number of societies, apprised of the spiritual, emotional, and physical state of the members. This helped assure that class members and their leaders received the care and encouragement they needed to grow in grace.

Regular meetings with the minister also assured that the leaders were not abusing their power. Those who were not doing their job were removed and replaced with more-suitable candidates. Those leaders who were faithful to their ministry received the support and encouragement they needed from the minister and from their fellow class leaders. Class leaders were powerful people, and accountability with their peers helped assure that their power was used for "building up the body of Christ" and not for personal pride (Ephesians 4:12).

Class leaders were extraordinary people who responded to God's grace and the invitation to leadership among their peers. Wesley regarded them with the highest regard. Consequently, he also placed high expectations on them and their ministry. Those who did not or could not measure up were removed from leadership. Those who possessed the gifts and graces needed were praised and supported. Many of them went on to become ministers. Class leaders were the men and women responsible for the effectiveness of the Methodist movement. They provided the day-to-day, week-to-week continuity, example, and leadership in discipleship for the rank-and-file members. The people could look to their class leaders as role models in faith and could count on them for spiritual and emotional care and support in times of need and distress.

Because most of the early Methodists came from among the working poor who led lives of quiet desperation in a world undergoing massive social transformation, the class leaders provided a place of refuge. The refuge (class meeting) had power to transform their hopelessness into hope because it had a mission and a structure they could hold onto as a guide for living. While the world around them was often chaotic and violent, the Methodists could look to their class and class leader as a source of direction and meaning for living. The class leaders were responsible for providing guidance and care for that refuge of peace in which people who often felt lost and alone could experience belonging and purpose for living.

Because of the faithfulness of many class leaders, innumerable people were given the means and habits they needed to lift themselves and their families out of grinding poverty. They were changed from understanding themselves as being nobodies into believing they were somebodies. They went from being nameless to knowing they belonged to God, who called them by name (Isaiah 43:1). Their class meeting gave them an identity. This could happen only under the faithful, Christ-led leadership of the class leaders.

Class leaders were like the section leaders of an orchestra. They made sure that everyone was present and accounted for, and that they learned and played the music as it was meant to be played. They helped those who were having difficulty learning their parts until they gained the skill and confidence they needed to play along with the rest of the section. Without the section leaders, the conductor would have to look after each member of each section (strings, brass, woodwinds, percussion) and do all the work the leaders do for him or her. There would be less time for rehearsal because the conductor would be running around making sure each section was doing its job. The section leaders enable the conductor to concentrate on conducting. With a skilled cadre of leaders and a talented conductor, an orchestra will make beautiful music that lifts the spirit and praises God.

Biblical Basis for Class Leaders

The office of class leader has its origins in Scripture. If it were not grounded in Scripture, it would not have enjoyed the import or power for transforming lives that history has witnessed. We will briefly look at two passages of Scripture to support the employment of class leaders: Exodus 18:13-27 and Acts 6:1-6.

Exodus 18:13-27 tells the story of Jethro, Moses' father-in-law, visiting Moses and the people in the wilderness. He observed that the people surrounded Moses "from morning until evening." Moses spent all of his time resolving disputes, interpreting the law for them, and teaching the "instructions of God" among the people. Jethro saw that Moses would soon burn out if he continued to keep this responsibility to himself, so he suggested an alternative that would spread out the responsibility. He told Moses he needed to delegate some authority to others who were "trustworthy...and hate dishonest gain."

> Let them sit as judges for the people at all times; let them bring every important case to you, but decide every minor case themselves. So it will be easier for you, and they will bear the burden with you. If you do this, and God so commands you, then you will be able to endure, and all these people will go to their home in peace.   (Exodus 18:22-23)

Moses, who must have been physically and emotionally exhausted, agreed. He appointed "able men from all Israel" to share in the care of the people.

Those able men helped Moses bear the responsibility for the pastoral care of the people of Israel in the wilderness. In sharing his pastoral power with other trustworthy people, Moses was able to spread out the workload, so that the needs of the people were met more effectively. The leaders appointed by Moses were given authority to settle minor disputes and to care for the everyday needs of the people. This meant that people no longer had to wait for an appointment with Moses; they could simply go to the leader sent by Moses to serve them. Only the difficult cases were brought to Moses, which freed him to dedicate more time to his calling as the prophet and shepherd for the people. It also made him a more effective spiritual leader and pastor.

In Acts 6:1-6, the apostles faced a situation similar to Moses' situation: "Now during those days, when the disciples were increasing in number, the Hellenists complained against the Hebrews because their widows were being neglected in the daily distribution of food" (Acts 6:1). The Christian community had grown to the point where the apostles could no longer effectively provide for the needs of the people. This led to a division between the Hellenists (Gentile Christians) and the Hebrews (Jewish Christians) and the perception among the Hellenists that the most vulnerable among them were not receiving their share of the community's resources. The apostles' response was a division of labor. They appointed seven men to be responsible for serving the tables and assuring that the needs of the widows were no longer neglected.

> And the twelve called together the whole community of the disciples and said, "It is not right that we should neglect the word of God in order to wait on tables. Therefore, friends, select from among yourselves seven men of good standing, full of the Spirit and of wisdom, whom we may appoint to this task, while we, for our part, will devote ourselves to prayer and to serving the word." (Acts 6:2-4)

Here, the whole community participated in choosing those who would serve them. Like the Israelites, the ones chosen to be leaders among them were to be people of "good standing, full of the Spirit and of wisdom." These deacons provided the daily care of the people while the apostles were free to devote themselves more fully to "serving the word." In other words, the deacons ministered to the daily tasks of visiting the widows and serving the tables. This freed the apostles to devote more time to their calling of preaching and teaching the good news of God in Jesus Christ. Again, the pastoral needs of the people were more effectively and faithfully met by a division of labor and the sharing of pastoral power.

The structure of the Methodist societies was similar to the organization of the Israelites in the wilderness (Exodus 18) and of the early church in Jerusalem (Acts 6). The preachers (or ministers) were responsible for the overall care of the societies to which they were appointed. Their primary responsibility was to preach the Word of God, administer the sacraments, and see to the care of the people. Because the preachers were itinerant, the class leaders were needed to see to the day-to-day needs of the people. They were like the deacons appointed by the community to wait on the tables and serve the widows in the early church. The class leaders were the ones who visited the sick and cared for the daily spiritual needs of the society. This division of labor and sharing of pastoral power and responsibility resulted in a most effective means of serving and caring for the people of God.

Stewards of Sanctification

What is the theological rationale for class leaders? The Wesleyan emphasis on sanctification and Christian perfection gave the office of class leader a highly significant role in the life of the Methodist society. People who were awakened to faith by grace needed a means of helping them live their faith. Prevenient grace awakened them to their sin and brought them to repentance. Justifying grace brought them into right relationship with God through faith in Jesus Christ. Through receiving Christ into their heart, they knew their sins were forgiven, they were God's beloved children, and, by sanctifying grace, they were set free to live the life God intended for them.

At the center of this new life were the General Rules:
- Do no harm, by avoiding evil of every kind.
- Do good, as often as you can to as many as you can.
- Attend to the ordinances of God (regular worship, studying and meditating on Scripture, the Lord's Supper, family and private prayer, and fasting or abstinence).

These rules were general because they were intended to serve not as law but as a rule for living. They are like a compass that helps a person stay on the course set for him or her by Jesus Christ. The class leader was the guide who helped people read and understand their compass and take a regular, weekly compass heading. This process of instruction and accountability, which was the hallmark of the class meeting, served to move people along in the process of sanctification. The General Rules enabled the Methodists to live out God's household rules: "You shall love the Lord your God with all your heart, and with all your soul, and with all your mind.... You shall love your neighbor as yourself" (Matthew 22:37, 39). Class leaders were among the people God provided to help people keep the household rules and grow in faith and go on to perfection in love.

Sanctification is the work of God in and with the community of faith. The process of being formed and conformed into the image of Christ requires the participation of those who submit to Christ and his will and those who are more seasoned, those who have had years of experience in Christian living. The class leaders were seasoned Christians who responded to Christ's call and took responsibility for the Christian formation of their sisters and brothers in Christ. They were stewards of sanctification. As they inquired into the state of the souls of their class members, advised, reproved, comforted, or exhorted them in the weekly meetings, the leaders helped people experience grace in their daily lives. They helped their brothers and sisters in Christ keep their hearts open to Christ's forming and reforming grace.

The class leaders also helped prevent the human tendency to self-deception. We humans work hard to justify and rationalize our sin. We are adept at deceiving ourselves into believing our known sins are excusable. The class leader and class meeting were the Wesleyan means of limiting this tendency toward self-deception. When people have to give an accounting of what they have and have not done, as happened in the class meeting, the possibility of self-deception is greatly reduced. It was the class leader's responsibility to help the members tell the story of their walk with Christ since their last meeting. When people gave such a weekly accounting of their discipleship, they were given a means for taking stock of the state of their soul. What they had done and left undone was revealed regularly for themselves. All this was done as a way for the leader and class to "watch over one another in love." Class leaders were stewards of sanctification because they were responsible for helping people along the way of sanctification through grace-filled, loving care.

Conclusion

If class leaders were so important and so necessary to the life of Methodists, why did they disappear? Class leaders did not disappear from all parts of Methodism. They continue to play a role in some African-American churches, as well as in Methodist churches outside the United States. They also have played a central role in the life and growth of the Korean Methodist Church. Nonetheless, class leaders essentially disappeared from the Methodist Episcopal Church (North and South) by the end of the nineteenth century.

Why? There are at least two reasons: the rise of station pastors and a desire on the part of the Methodists for respectability. The first occurred sometime in the 1840's, when the Methodist preachers began to dismount from their horses and stopped riding their circuits. Simultaneously, the church was experiencing rapid growth and felt the need for greater respectability. In their desire to be respectable, Methodists began to build impressive church buildings. When they had their buildings, they wanted pastors to serve and maintain them. The preachers stopped riding their circuits in order to serve the station churches.

When the pastors settled into communities, they began to take on many of the responsibilities of the class leaders. The pastors were expected to call on members, to visit the sick, to teach the children. As time went on, the role of the class leader diminished in favor of the clergy who were given more responsibilities and more power. The class meetings began to decline. The class leaders' power and responsibility was shifted more and more to the clergy. As the clergy became more powerful within congregations, they became reluctant to share power with the class leaders and other lay leaders.

Some class leaders became Sunday school teachers or trustees or took other leadership roles in the church. But the pastor absorbed their role as stewards of sanctification. The result of this unfortunate development was a marked decline in the emphasis on sanctification as the work of the church for its people and the world. The office of class leader became optional and, eventually, disposable.

The church needs class leaders today as much as, if not more than, it did 250 years ago. People today are hungry for God, and more and more are realizing and experiencing the emptiness of materialism, consumerism, and busyness. They are looking for a way to connect with others and with God. People in the church are hungry for opportunities to be in ministry and are looking for ways to employ the gifts God has given them to serve Christ in the world. Pastors are stretched to the limits with demands on their time and skills.

Reclaiming the tradition of class leaders would go a long way toward renewing the church by addressing the church's needs for support, encouragement, and accountability in its faith. Retraditioning the office of class leader also would relieve pastors, whose time and energy are stretched far too thin by the needs and administrative demands of the local church. If class leaders were deployed, pastoral responsibility and power would be spread throughout the congregation. This sharing of pastoral power also would make itinerancy more effective because the congregation, led by class leaders, would have much stronger ownership of its ministry and mission. With a cadre of faithful class leaders, the character of the life of a congregation likely would not shift substantially with each change in pastoral leadership. Pastors would need to work more collegially with the laity, and the church could function more as a team engaged in ministry than as a corporation led by a CEO. The pastor could devote more time to the work of his or her calling—namely, preaching the good news of Christ, administering the sacraments, and equipping people for ministry.

Class leaders were stewards of sanctification. They were the section leaders, the noncommissioned officers, the mentors, and the coaches for the Methodist movement. They were the men and women who supported, nurtured, and led the people called Methodists in their walk with Christ. They provided the continuity of care and instruction the societies and churches needed when the preachers rode their circuits and were absent from their flocks for long periods. Class leaders were the people the Methodist Church needed for an itinerant ministry to work. Without the class leaders, the movement in England and the Methodist Church in America would never have survived and thrived. Class leaders were the ones who supported the preachers in their ministry of proclaiming the Word and administering the sacraments. They provided the pastoral care and leadership for their neighbors that helped many of them claim and live their faith in Christ. The office of class leader is a great gift that the church today needs to reclaim.

For Reflection and Discussion

1. Who were the class leaders?
2. What did class leaders do?
3. Why were the class leaders so important to the Methodist movement?
4. Would you consider becoming a class leader?
5. How could class leaders expand the pastoral ministry of your church?
6. Are there people in your church you think would make good class leaders?

To Learn More

Guide for Class Leaders: A Model for Christian Formation, by Grace Bradford (Nashville: Discipleship Resources, 1999).

John Wesley's Class Meeting: A Model for Making Disciples, by D. Michael Henderson (Nappanee, IN: Evangel Publishing House, 1997).

The Radical Wesley: And Patterns for Church Renewal, by Howard A. Snyder (Grand Rapids: Zondervan Publishing House, 1987).

They Walked in the Spirit: Personal Faith and Social Action in America, by Douglas M. Strong (Louisville: Westminster John Knox Press, 1997).

Wesley and Sanctification: A Study in the Doctrine of Salvation, by Harald Lindström (Nappanee, IN: Evangel Publishing House, second edition 1996).

(Books from Discipleship Resources can be ordered through the online bookstore, http://www.discipleshipresources.org, or by phone, 800-685-4370.)

Epilogue

Accountable Discipleship: Now What?

The obvious question to ask at the conclusion of this book is, "So what? This all sounds well and good, but what does it have to do with me?" The best response to this question is personal testimony from people whose lives have been transformed by their experience with Accountable Discipleship. The class meeting and class leaders were organized by the Wesleys to meet the needs of people who were hungry for God. They were not academic exercises, nor were they short-term programs designed to help people study the Bible and learn about discipleship. The class meetings and class leaders grew out of a need to help people grow in their relationship with Jesus Christ. And, like baptism, the relationship with Christ was, and remains, a lifetime commitment. The class meetings and class leaders were the structure and organization that helped people live out and grow in their relationship with Christ. They were places where people were transformed into disciples through love. They learned what it meant to love God wholeheartedly and to love their neighbor as themselves.

Covenant Discipleship Groups, which are found in congregations throughout The United Methodist Church, are today's adaptation of the Methodist class meeting. These groups and class leaders are forming people like you and me into faithful disciples of Jesus Christ in much the same way disciples were formed by the Wesleys in eighteenth-century England and America: through accountability and loving support (watching over one another in love).

During a recent visit to a United Methodist Church in Washington, D.C., I sat down with some class leaders. At the time, the church had fifteen Covenant Discipleship Groups and twenty-five class leaders. I asked each class leader what difference Accountable Discipleship had made in his or her life. Each class leader, who was a member of a Covenant Discipleship Group, had been commissioned by his or her church to be a class leader responsible for up to twenty families in the church. As class leaders, they kept in touch with the families, visited in their homes, and helped connect them to the church's ministry. They met once a month with the pastor to give an account of the ministry with their class members and to receive spiritual support. The ministry of class leaders carries great responsibility and challenges. The support and accountability from the Covenant Discipleship Groups, other class leaders, and the pastor equip the class leaders to be faithful discipleship leaders.

George told me that before he joined a Covenant Discipleship Group, he seldom read his Bible and saw Sunday morning worship as a chore to be endured once or twice a month. He did not contribute much of his time or gifts to the ministry of the church, but things began to change after one of the class leaders convinced him to join a Covenant Discipleship Group. Over time, George found himself reading the Bible almost daily. He eventually joined a DISCIPLE Bible study class and spent thirty-four weeks studying the whole of the Scriptures. Worship began to connect with his heart and mind to the point that he eventually began to volunteer to read Scripture and help serve the Lord's Supper. When his pastor told him that he thought he would make a good class leader, George did not say no. He agreed to give it a try. That was three years ago. George is now seen as a leader in the church. He is awed and humbled by the blessings God has given him each step along the way. He especially values the relationships he enjoys with his Covenant Discipleship Group and his fellow class leaders.

The only reason Gladys ever went to church on Sunday was to see who was there and who was not there. She liked to gossip and judge people based on to their appearance, especially the dresses, shoes, and hats the women were wearing. Church was a social occasion for her, and worship had little to do with God and everything to do with appearances and gossip. That was before Gladys accepted an invitation from one of the class leaders to join a Covenant Discipleship Group. At first she thought the group would be another occasion to get and exchange juicy gossip. But that did not last long, for the group's spirit began to change her. The love and acceptance she experienced, along with the responsibility of being accountable for her discipleship, caused her to see herself differently. For the first time in her life, Gladys saw herself as a child of God and the people around her as her brothers and sisters. After a while, her reasons for going to worship on Sunday mornings began to change. Her interest in gossiping about who was wearing what and who was in church began to diminish. Eventually, the only reason Gladys went to church on Sunday was to worship God. Her Covenant Discipleship Group had helped her live as a child of God in God's household.

Helen had a problem with homeless people. She did not like to be around them because she was offended by their appearance and smell. Homeless people were a regular presence on the sidewalk outside her inner-city church, which was in a lower-income neighborhood. When she encountered them on Sunday morning, she did her best to ignore them and keep walking until she was safely inside the church. Helen regarded those unfortunate souls as being something less than human and not worthy of her attention or care.

Like George and Gladys, Helen began to change soon after she accepted her pastor's invitation to join a Covenant Discipleship Group. In her covenant she promised to read the Bible, pray every day, and serve in the church's outreach to the homeless and poor people in the neighborhood. Her group gave her unconditional love and support through the struggle to confront her fear of homeless people. Eventually, by the grace of mutual support and accountability, Helen's heart was changed. One Sunday she was stopped on her way to church by a homeless man who asked her for spare change. Rather than hurry past him she stopped, reached in her purse, and pulled out a five-dollar bill. She placed it in the man's hand, looked into his eyes, and said, "God bless and keep you." For the first time she was able to see Christ in the face of a homeless man. Today she makes sure she has money and a smile to give to those she encounters on the street who need them. She also is involved in the church's feeding program and outreach to the men, women, and families who live on the streets of Washington, D.C. Helen is now a class leader.

The mutual accountability and support of Covenant Discipleship Groups helps remove the blockages to grace. The trust that is built, the love that is shared, and the process of accountability for discipleship help grace flow through the lives of group members. In the process, as people practice the means of grace in their daily lives, blockages to grace are removed from the life of the congregation. The mission and ministry of the church is strengthened and the church grows spiritually.

Accountable Discipleship, when it is incorporated into the bloodstream of a congregation, empowers and equips the church to become the household of God. It transforms lives by helping men and women, boys and girls understand who and whose they are. It provides the structure that empowers them to live as children of God and members of God's household. Covenant Discipleship Groups provide the mutual accountability and support that people need to keep the household rules (love God and love your neighbor as yourself) and follow Jesus Christ as he works to bring all of God's children into the household of faith.

For Reflection and Discussion

1. If you are a member of a Covenant Discipleship Group, how is your group like a class meeting? How is it different?
2. If you are not in a Covenant Discipleship Group, is it something that you think would help you become more accountable in your discipleship? If you are interested in joining or starting a Covenant Discipleship Group, talk with your pastor.

To Learn More

Covenant Discipleship Quarterly, a quarterly newsletter for members of Covenant Discipleship Groups, can be found on the General Board of Discipleship Web site (http://www.gbod.org/smallgroup/covenant/default.html).

Guide for Covenant Discipleship Groups, by Gayle Turner Watson (Nashville: Discipleship Resources, 2000).

Sprouts: Nurturing Children Through Covenant Discipleship, by Edie Genung Harris and Shirley L. Ramsey (Nashville: Discipleship Resources, 1995).

Together in Love: Covenant Discipleship With Youth, by David C. Sutherland (Nashville: Discipleship Resources, 1999).

(Books from Discipleship Resources can be ordered through the online bookstore, http://www.discipleshipresources.org, or by phone, 800-685-4370.)

Appendix

The Scripture Way of Salvation

(Ephesians 2:8: "Ye are saved through faith.")

by John Wesley

1. Nothing can be more intricate, complex, and hard to be understood, than religion as it has been often described. And this is not only true concerning the religion of the heathens, even many of the wisest of them, but concerning the religion of those also who were in some sense Christians; yea, and men of great name in the Christian world, men "who seemed to be pillars" thereof. Yet how easy to be understood, how plain and simple a thing, is the genuine religion of Jesus Christ! Provided only that we take it in its native form, just as it is described in the oracles of God. It is exactly suited by the wise Creator and Governor of the world to the weak understanding and narrow capacity of man in his present state. How observable is this both with regard to the end it proposes and the means to attain that end! The end is, in one word, salvation: the means to attain it, faith.

2. It is easily discerned that these two little words—I mean faith and salvation—include the substance of all the Bible, the marrow, as it were, of the whole Scripture. So much the more should we take all possible care to avoid all mistake concerning them, and to form a true and accurate judgment concerning both the one and the other.

   Let us then seriously inquire,
   I. What is salvation?
   II. What is that faith whereby we are saved? And
   III. How we are saved by it?

I.

1. And first let us inquire, What is *salvation*? The salvation which is here spoken of is not what is frequently understood by that word, the going to heaven, eternal happiness. It is not the soul's going to paradise, termed by our Lord "Abraham's bosom." It is not a blessing which lies on the other side death, or (as we usually speak) in the other world. The very words of the text itself put this beyond all question. "Ye *are* saved." It is not something at a distance: it is a present thing, a blessing which, through the free mercy of God, ye are now in possession of. Nay, the words may be rendered, and that with equal propriety, "Ye *have been* saved." So that the salvation which is here spoken of might be extended to the entire work of God, from the first dawning of grace in the soul till it is consummated in glory.

2. If we take this in its utmost extent it will include all that is wrought in the soul by what is frequently termed "natural conscience," but more properly, "preventing grace"; all the "drawings" of "the Father," the desires after God, which, if we yield to them, increase more and more; all that "light" wherewith the Son of God "enlighteneth everyone that cometh into the world," *showing* every man "to do justly, to love mercy, and to walk humbly with his God"; all the *convictions* which his Spirit from time to time works in every child of man. Although it is true the generality of men stifle them as soon as possible, and after a while forget, or at least deny, that ever they had them at all.

3. But we are at present concerned only with that salvation which the Apostle is directly speaking of. And this consists of two general parts, justification and sanctification.

   Justification is another word for pardon. It is the forgiveness of all our sins, and (what is necessarily implied therein) our acceptance with God. The price whereby this hath been procured for us (commonly termed the "meritorious cause" of our justification) is the blood and righteousness of Christ, or (to express it a little more clearly) all that Christ hath done and suffered for us till "he poured out his soul for the transgressors." The immediate effects of justification are, the peace of God, a "peace that passeth all understanding," and a "rejoicing in *hope* of the glory of God," "with *joy* unspeakable and full of glory."

4. And at the same time that we are justified, yea, in that very moment, *sanctification* begins. In that instant we are "born again," "born from above," "born of the Spirit." There is a *real* as well as a *relative* change. We are inwardly renewed by the power of God. We feel the "love of God shed abroad in our heart by the Holy Ghost which is given unto us," producing love to all mankind, and more especially to the children of God; expelling the love of the world, the love of pleasure, of ease, of honour, of money; together with pride, anger, self-will, and every other evil

temper—in a word, changing the "earthly, sensual, devilish" mind into "the mind which was in Christ Jesus."

5. How naturally do those who experience such a change imagine that all sin is gone! That it is utterly rooted out of their heart, and has no more any place therein! How easily do they draw that inference, "I *feel* no sin; therefore I *have* none." It does not *stir;* therefore it does not *exist:* It has no *motion;* therefore it has no *being.*

6. But it is seldom long before they are undeceived, finding sin was only suspended, not destroyed. Temptations return and sin revives, showing it was but stunned before, not dead. They now feel two principles in themselves, plainly contrary to each other: "the flesh lusting against the spirit," nature opposing the grace of God. They cannot deny that although they still feel power to believe in Christ and to love God, and although his "Spirit" still "witnesses with" their "spirits that" they "are the children of God"; yet they feel in themselves, sometimes pride or self-will, sometimes anger or unbelief. They find one or more of these frequently *stirring* in their heart, though not *conquering;* yea, perhaps "thrusting sore at them that they" may "fall; but the Lord is" their "help."

7. How exactly did Macarius, fourteen hundred years ago, describe the present experience of the children of God! "The unskillful (or unexperienced), when grace operates, presently imagine they have no more sin. Whereas they that have discretion cannot deny that even we who have the grace of God may be molested again.... For we have often had instances of some among the brethren who have experienced such grace as to affirm that they had no sin in them. And yet after all, when they thought themselves entirely freed from it, the corruption that lurked within was stirred up anew, and they were wellnigh burnt up."

8. From the time of our being "born again" the gradual work of sanctification takes place. We are enabled "by the Spirit" to "mortify the deeds of the body," of our evil nature. And as we are more and more dead to sin, we are more and more alive to God. We go on from grace to grace, while we are careful to "abstain from all appearance of evil," and are "zealous of good works," "as we have opportunity doing good to all men"; while we walk in all His ordinances blameless, therein worshipping him in spirit and in truth; while we take up our cross and deny ourselves every pleasure that does not lead us to God.

9. It is thus that we wait for entire sanctification, for a full salvation from all our sins, from pride, self-will, anger, unbelief, or, as the Apostle expresses it, "Go on to perfection." But what is perfection? The word has various senses: here it means perfect love. It is love excluding sin; love filling the heart, taking up the whole capacity of the soul. It is love "rejoicing evermore, praying without ceasing, in everything giving thanks."

II. But what is that "faith through which we are saved"? This is the second point to be considered.

1. Faith in general is defined by the Apostle,...—"an evidence," a divine "evidence and conviction" (the word means both), "of things not seen"—not visible, not perceivable either by sight or by any other of the external senses. It implies both a supernatural *evidence* of God and of the things of God, a kind of spiritual *light* exhibited to the soul, and a supernatural *sight* or perception thereof. Accordingly the Scripture speaks sometimes of God's giving light, sometimes a power of discerning it. So St. Paul: "God, who commanded light to shine out of darkness, hath shined in our hearts, to give us the light of the knowledge of the glory of God in the face of Jesus Christ." And elsewhere the same Apostle speaks "of the eyes of" our "understanding being opened." By this twofold operation of the Holy Spirit—having the eyes of our soul both *opened* and *enlightened*—we see the things which the natural "eye hath not seen, neither the ear heard." We have a prospect of the invisible things of God. We see the *spiritual world,* which is all round about us, and yet no more discerned by our natural faculties than if it had no being; and we see the *eternal world,* piercing through the veil which hangs between time and eternity. Clouds and darkness then rest upon it no more, but we already see the glory which shall be revealed.

2. Taking the word in a more particular sense, faith is a divine evidence and conviction, not only that "God was in Christ, reconciling the world unto himself," but also that Christ "loved *me,* and gave himself for *me.*" It is by this faith (whether we term it the *essence,* or rather a *property* thereof) that we "receive Christ"; that we receive him in all his offices, as our Prophet, Priest, and King. It is by this that he "is made of God unto us wisdom, and righteousness, and sanctification, and redemption."

3. "But is this the 'faith of assurance' or 'faith of adherence'?" The Scripture mentions no such distinction. The Apostle says: "There is one faith, and one hope of our calling," one Christian, saving faith, as "there is one Lord" in whom we believe, and "one God and Father of us all." And it is certain this faith necessarily implies an *assurance* (which is here only another word for *evidence,* it being hard to tell the difference between them) that "Christ loved *me,* and gave himself for *me.*" For "he that believeth" with the true, living faith, "hath the witness in himself." "The Spirit witnesseth with his spirit that he is a child of God." "Because he is a son, God hath sent forth the Spirit of his Son into his heart, crying, Abba, Father," giving him an assurance that he is so, and a childlike confidence in him. But let it be observed that, in the very nature of the thing, the assurance goes before the confidence. For a man cannot have a childlike confidence in God till he knows he is a child of God. Therefore confidence, trust, reliance, adherence, or whatever else it be called, is not the first, as some have supposed, but the second branch or act of faith.

4. It is by this faith we "are saved," justified and sanctified, taking that word in its highest sense. But how are we justified and sanctified by faith? This is our third head of inquiry. And this being the main point in question, and a point of no ordinary importance, it will not be improper to give it a more distinct and particular consideration.

III.

1. And first, how are we justified by faith? In what sense is this to be understood? I answer, faith is the condition, and the only condition, of justification. It is the condition: none is justified but he that believes; without faith no man is justified. And it is the only condition: this alone is sufficient for justification. Everyone that believes is justified, whatever else he has or has not. In other words: no man is justified till he believes; every man when he believes is justified.

2. "But does not God command us to *repent* also? Yea, and to 'bring forth fruits meet for repentance'? To 'cease,' for instance, 'from doing evil,' and 'learn to do well'? And is not both the one and the other of the utmost necessity? Insomuch that if we willingly neglect either we cannot reasonably expect to be justified at all? But if this be so, how can it be said that faith is the only condition of justification?"

God does undoubtedly command us both to repent and to bring forth fruits meet for repentance; which if we willingly neglect we cannot reasonably expect to be justified at all. Therefore both repentance and fruits meet for repentance are in some sense necessary to justification. But they are not necessary in the *same sense* with faith, nor in the *same degree.* Not in the *same degree;* for those fruits are only necessary *conditionally,* if there be time and opportunity for them. Otherwise a man may be justified without them, as was the "thief" upon the cross (if we may call him so; for a late writer has discovered that he was no thief, but a very honest and respectable person!) But he cannot be justified without faith: this is impossible. Likewise let a man have ever so much repentance, or ever so many of the fruits meet for repentance, yet all this does not at all avail: he is not justified till he believes. But the moment he believes, with or without those fruits, yea, with more or less repentance, he is justified. Not in the *same sense:* for repentance and its fruits are only *remotely* necessary, necessary in order to faith; whereas faith is *immediately* and *directly* necessary to justification. It remains that faith is the only condition which is *immediately* and *proximately* necessary to justification.

3. "But do you believe we are sanctified by faith? We know you believe that we are justified by faith; but do not you believe, and accordingly teach, that we are sanctified by our works?"

So it has been roundly and vehemently affirmed for these five and twenty years. But I have constantly declared just the contrary, and that in all manner of ways. I have continually testified in private and in public that we are sanctified, as well as justified, by faith. And indeed the one of these great truths does exceedingly illustrate the other. Exactly as we are justified by faith, so are we sanctified by faith. Faith is the condition, and the only condition of sanctification, exactly as it is of justification. It is the condition: none is sanctified but he that believes; without faith no man is sanctified. And it is the only condition: this alone is sufficient for sanctification. Everyone that believes is sanctified, whatever else he has or has not. In other words: no man is sanctified till he believes; every man when he believes is sanctified.

4. "But is there not a repentance consequent upon, as well as a repentance previous to, justification? And is it not incumbent on all that are justified to be 'zealous of good works'? Yea, are not these so necessary that if a man willingly neglect them he cannot reasonably expect that he shall ever be sanctified in the full sense, that is, 'perfected in love'? Nay, can he 'grow' at all 'in grace, in the' loving 'knowledge of our Lord Jesus Christ'? Yea, can he retain the grace which God has already given him? Can he continue in the faith which he has received, or in the favour of God? Do not you yourself allow all this, and continually assert it? But if this be so, how can it be said that faith is the only condition of sanctification?"

5. I do allow all this, and continually maintain it as the truth of God. I allow there is a repentance consequent upon, as well as a repentance previous to, justification. It is incumbent on all that are justified to be zealous of good works. And these are so necessary that if a man willingly neglect them, he cannot reasonably expect that he shall ever be sanctified. He cannot "grow in grace," in the image of God, the mind which was in Christ Jesus; nay, he cannot retain the grace he has received, he cannot continue in faith, or in the favour of God.

What is the inference we must draw herefrom? Why, that both repentance, rightly understood, and the practice of all good works, works of piety, as well as works of mercy (now properly so called, since they spring from faith) are in some sense necessary to sanctification.

6. I say "repentance rightly understood"; for this must not be confounded with the former repentance. The repentance consequent upon justification is widely different from that which is antecedent to it. This implies no guilt, no sense of condemnation, no consciousness of the wrath of God. It does not suppose any doubt of the favour of God, or any "fear that hath torment." It is properly a conviction wrought by the Holy Ghost of the "sin" which still "remains" in our heart; of..."the carnal mind," which "does still *remain*," as our Church speaks, "even in them that are regenerate"—although it does no longer *reign*, it has not now dominion over them. It is a conviction of our proneness to evil, of an heart "bent to backsliding" of the still continuing tendency of the "flesh" to "lust against the Spirit." Sometimes, unless we continually watch and pray, it lusteth to pride, sometimes to anger, sometimes to love of the world, love of ease,

love of honour, or love of pleasure more than of God. It is a conviction of the tendency of our heart to self-will, to atheism, or idolatry; and above all to unbelief, whereby in a thousand ways, and under a thousand pretences, we are ever "departing" more or less "from the living God."

7. With this conviction of the sin *remaining* in our hearts there is joined a clear conviction of the sin remaining in our lives, still *cleaving* to all our words and actions. In the best of these we now discern a mixture of evil, either in the spirit, the matter, or the manner of them; something that could not endure the righteous judgment of God, were he "extreme to mark what is done amiss." Where we least suspected it we find a taint of pride of self-will, of unbelief or idolatry; so that we are now more ashamed of our best duties than formerly of our worst sins. And hence we cannot but feel that these are so far from having anything meritorious in them, yea, so far from being able to stand in sight of the divine justice, that for those also we should be guilty before God were it not for the blood of the covenant.

8. Experience shows that together with this conviction of sin *remaining* in our hearts and *cleaving* to all our words and actions, as well as the guilt which on account thereof we should incur were we not continually sprinkled with the atoning blood, one thing more is implied in this repentance, namely, a conviction of our helplessness, of our utter inability to think one good thought, or to form one good desire; and much more to speak one word aright, or to perform one good action but through his free, almighty grace, first preventing us, and then accompanying us every moment.

9. "But what good works are those, the practice of which you affirm to be necessary to sanctification?" First, all works of piety, such as public prayer, family prayer, and praying in our closet; receiving the Supper of the Lord; searching the Scriptures by hearing, reading, meditating; and using such a measure of fasting or abstinence as our bodily health allows.

10. Secondly, all works of mercy, whether they relate to the bodies or souls of men; such as feeding the hungry, clothing the naked, entertaining the stranger, visiting those that are in prison, or sick, or variously afflicted; such as the endeavouring to instruct the ignorant, to awaken the stupid sinner, to quicken the lukewarm, to confirm the wavering, to comfort the feeble-minded, to succour the tempted, or contribute in any manner to the saving of souls from death. This is the repentance, and these the fruits meet for repentance, which are necessary to full sanctification. This is the way wherein God hath appointed his children to wait for complete salvation.

11. Hence may appear the extreme mischievousness of that seemingly innocent opinion that "there is no sin in a believer; that all sin is destroyed, root and branch, the moment a man is justified." By totally preventing that repentance it quite blocks up the way to sanctification. There is no place for repentance in him who believes there is no sin either in his life or heart. Consequently there is no place for his being "perfected in love," to which that repentance is indispensably necessary.

12. Hence it may likewise appear that there is no possible danger in *thus* expecting full salvation. For suppose we were mistaken, suppose no such blessing ever was or can be attained, yet we lose nothing. Nay, that very expectation quickens us in using all the talents which God has given us; yea, in improving them all, so that when our Lord cometh he will "receive his own with increase."

13. But to return. Though it be allowed that both this repentance and its fruits are necessary to full salvation, yet they are not necessary either in the *same sense* with faith or in the *same degree.* Not in the same degree; for these fruits are only necessary *conditionally,* if there be time and opportunity for them. Otherwise a man may be sanctified without them. But he cannot be sanctified without faith. Likewise let a man have ever so much of this repentance, or ever so many good works, yet all this does not at all avail: he is not sanctified till he believes. But the moment he believes, with or without those fruits, yea, with more or less of this repentance, he is sanctified. Not in the *same sense;* for this repentance and these fruits are only *remotely* necessary, necessary in order to the continuance of his faith, as well as the increase of it; whereas faith is *immediately* and *directly* necessary to sanctification. It remains that faith is the only condition which is *immediately* and *proximately* necessary to sanctification.

14. "But what is that faith whereby we are sanctified, saved from sin and perfected in love?" It is a divine evidence and conviction, first, that God hath promised it in the Holy Scripture. Till we are thoroughly satisfied of this there is no moving one step farther. And one would imagine there needed not one word more to satisfy a reasonable man of this than the ancient promise, "Then will I circumcise thy heart, and the heart of thy seed, to love the Lord your God with all your heart, and with all your soul." How clearly does this express the being perfected in love! How strongly imply the being saved from all sin! For as long as love takes up the whole heart, what room is there for sin therein?

15. It is a divine evidence and conviction, secondly, that what God hath promised he is *able* to perform. Admitting therefore that "with men it is impossible" to bring a clean thing out of an unclean, to purify the heart from all sin, and to fill it with all holiness, yet this creates no difficulty in the case, seeing "with God all things are possible." And surely no one ever imagined it was possible to any power less than that of the Almighty! But if God speaks, it shall be done. God saith, "Let there be light: and there is light."

16. It is, thirdly, a divine evidence and conviction that he is able and willing to do it *now.* And why not? Is not a moment to him the same as a thousand years? He cannot want more time to accomplish whatever is his will. And he cannot want or stay for any more *worthiness* or *fitness* in the persons he is pleased to honour. We may therefore boldly say, at any point of time, "Now is the day of salvation." "*Today* if ye will hear his voice, harden not your hearts." "Behold! all things are now ready! Come unto the marriage!"

17. To this confidence, that God is both able and willing to sanctify us *now*, there needs to be added one thing more, a divine evidence and conviction that *he doth it*. In that hour it is done. God says to the inmost soul, "According to thy faith be it unto thee!" Then the soul is pure from every spot of sin; "it is clean from all unrighteousness." The believer then experiences the deep meaning of those solemn words, "If we walk in the light, as he is in the light, we have fellowship one with another, and the blood of Jesus Christ his Son cleanseth us from all sin."

18. "But does God work this great work in the soul *gradually* or *instantaneously?*" Perhaps it may be gradually wrought in some. I mean in this sense—they do not advert to the particular moment wherein sin ceases to be. But it is infinitely desirable, were it the will of God, that it should be done instantaneously; that the Lord should destroy sin "by the breath of his mouth" in a moment, in the twinkling of an eye. And so he generally does, a plain fact of which there is evidence enough to satisfy any unprejudiced person. *Thou* therefore look for it every moment. Look for it in the way above described; in all those "good works" whereunto thou art "created anew in Christ Jesus." There is then no danger. You can be no worse, if you are no better for that expectation. For were you to be disappointed of your hope, still you lose nothing. But you shall not be disappointed of your hope: it will come, and will not tarry. Look for it then every day, every hour, every moment. Why not this hour, this moment? Certainly you may look for it *now,* if you believe it is by faith. And by this token may you surely know whether you seek it by faith or by works. If by works, you want something to be done *first, before* you are sanctified. You think, "I must first *be* or *do* thus or thus." Then you are seeking it by works unto this day. If you seek it by faith, you may expect it *as you are:* and if as you are, then expect it *now.* It is of importance to observe that there is an inseparable connection between these three points—expect it *by faith,* expect it *as you are,* and expect it *now!* To deny one of them is to deny them all: to allow one is to allow them all. Do *you* believe we are sanctified by faith? Be true then to your principle, and look for this blessing just as you are, neither better, nor worse; as a poor sinner that has still nothing to pay, nothing to plead but "Christ died." And if you look for it as you are, then expect it *now.* Stay for nothing. Why should you? Christ is ready. And he is all you want. He is waiting for you. He is at the door! Let your inmost soul cry out,

> Come in, come in, thou heavenly Guest!
>   Nor hence again remove:
> But sup with me, and let the feast
>   Be everlasting love.

(From "The Scripture Way of Salvation," in *The Works of John Wesley,* Volume 2, edited by Albert C. Outler, pages 155–69. © 1985 Abingdon Press. Used by permission.)